SHIT HAPPENS

Creating Your Plan to Survive and Thrive When Faced with Life's Personal and Natural Disasters

Linda O Fostek

Parker House Publishing
www.ParkerHouseBooks.com

Editing: AroundTheWritersTable.com
Book design and production: ParkerHouseBooks.com

First Printing June 2015

What People Are Saying About Shit Happens

I knew the moment that I looked at the Table of Contents that "S*** Happens" was an absolute treasure! Thanks to Linda Fostek for putting all of this essential information into one, easy-to-use handbook that will have a prominent place on my bookshelf. Though I think of myself as a careful planner, there was much in this book that I had not considered and I am thankful to now have this information close at hand.

Although I anticipated the wealth of information, what I did not expect was the feeling I had after reading this book. I felt capable, competent, and cared for. The warm, personal tone of the book avoids preaching, judgment, and rules and instead leaves the reader with the sense of having a personal disaster advisor who will always be ready with the solutions that take the drama out of disaster. I imagine this is just the feeling that the author had when her father was first dispensing some of this advice many years ago.

Every home should have a copy of this important book.

—**Gail Dixon**, Speaker, Author, Coach and CEO
Mastering Authentic Change

Linda Fostek has addressed a series of tough to discuss topics related to taking control of the future by being prepared in the present. As uncomfortable as most families are discussing the possibility of loss of job, life, home, or family, it is both important and necessary. As a retired School Superintendent and emergency service provider in both EMS and Fire-Rescue, I hear all too often, "What am I supposed to do now?" All emergency service professionals understand that the time for preparation and planning is way before the incident occurs. Linda has outlined a multitude of possible crises from small to large and a series of steps and resources that, if used in advance, can eliminate much of the emotional pain that typically results. Whether you are single or married, at the beginning or end of a career, have a large extended family or none at all, you will find problems and resources that will help you take control.

—**Alan B. Groveman**, Ed.D, Fire Department Captain,
Ambulance Corps Assistant Chief

As a para-medic and firefighter I often see people on the worst day of their lives. Shit Happens is a valuable resource to assist you in creating your disaster plan. If you don't know where to begin you will be guided through the process step by step. You will be assisted in identifying, creating and gathering your important papers that are essential to address any crisis you may face to minimize the impact on you and your family

—**Zack Matthews**, Paramedic-Firefighter

DEDICATION

To the most amazing person I have ever known.
His insatiable curiosity was rivaled
only by his zest for life.
To the man who taught me
that every problem has a solution.
That planning for success, combined with
consistent effort, will be rewarded.
To the one who dared me to reach for the stars
and showed me that dreams can come true,
this book is a tribute to your legacy.
I have been blessed to call you
My father . . .

Norbert Osiecki
6-12-1922 to 9-6-2012

ABOUT THE AUTHOR

I have been a planner for as long as I can remember. I plan for travel like it is an expedition. When I go scuba diving, oftentimes it is. Traveling to remote islands in the Pacific taught me to anticipate what can possibly go wrong. Things you take for granted at home may not be available somewhere else. You have to carry a first aid kit, antibiotics, ear medicine, and even a suture kit. You may be sleeping under the stars, or your hotel could have limited running water or power outages.

I always listen to storm warnings for hurricanes and blizzards. I watch the weather reports to see what the week looks like. I make lists and check things off.

I always try to anticipate what can happen. Have I prepared for storms that never came? Yes, I have. Did I get upset about it? Never. I've always felt that it is better to be prepared than sorry. I look at the bright side of the story. If a hurricane is predicted for Labor Day Weekend, I pack away all the outdoor furniture and, if nothing happens, I am prepared for the winter, just a week or two early. I have no regrets for doing the preparation because it is about protecting my property from damage and people from possible injury.

I have carefully planned my financial future. I invested well and contributed to my 401K account. I put my legal documents in place in my forties and made sure I had the insurance I needed to protect my husband in the event something happened to me.

My father, Norbert Osiecki, was a planner too. He built his home one concrete block and one nail at a time, following World War II. The home was modified, upgraded, and expanded to meet the changing needs of the family. There was nothing he could not build or repair.

Road trips were carefully mapped out—what to see, where to stay, and how far to drive every day. The last trip we took together took us from Calgary, Canada, to Albuquerque, New Mexico. We traveled thirty-three hundred miles in fifteen days. He was eighty-seven years old at the time. He planned for his life and his future. He taught me well.

In addition to being a planner, my dad constantly sought solutions for problems he saw in his own life and in the lives of others. At seventy, he realized that many of his friends were losing either a husband or wife. He saw the chaos this created for the surviving spouse. After fifty or sixty years of marriage, not only did the survivor suffer a profound emotional loss. A helplessness also arose from a lack of knowledge about certain tasks.

A marriage of that length often led to a division of labor that was comfortable. One spouse may have handled all the finances leaving the other in the dark about income, expenses, and investments. One may have handled the inside of the house while the other took care of the outside. The home was no longer a comfortable cocoon as the husband struggled to use the washing machine, or the wife was faced with a leak in the basement.

He decided to write a book that would organize all the information in one place and also be a home operations manual. He completed it, but he failed to market the concept successfully.

Twenty years later, I met Loral Langemeier, "The Millionaire Maker," and Keven Harrington, creator of the "As Seen on TV" brand, at an event. They inspired me to think about my father's project in a whole new way. I embraced his vision of helping others cope with disasters in their lives. I envisioned his manual updated and repackaged for the 21st century. I am committed to bringing his vision to life. I feel his presence guiding me and encouraging me every step of the way.

This book is but the first part of a bigger vision called *The Crisis Planner*.

My father passed away in 2012 at the age of ninety. He was still creating solutions to problems right up until he died. He is my inspiration and my guiding light.

This project is a tribute to the great man who taught me the importance and value of a good plan. He taught me the value of taking action and seeing a project to completion. He taught me to believe all things are possible.

I am proud to be his daughter and prouder still to bring his legacy to life.

Linda O Fostek

SOMETHING TO THINK ABOUT...

Having a plan for disaster is not enough.

Having the right plan in place prior to a disaster is critical.

Case in point -

The river water rose fast and the homeowner was forced to climb onto his roof. While standing in the rain and howling wind, a man in a rowboat approached the homeowner and invited him to get into the boat. The man declined the offer, responding, "The Lord will save me." The man in the rowboat left to see if there was anyone else in need of rescue.

The rain continued and the river kept rising. Now the man was forced to climb to the peak of his roof. His footing was wobbly and he had to bend over to keep hold on the roof.

Three men in a rubber raft approached him and offered him a ride to safety. Once again, the man clinging to the roof declined the offer, responding, "The Lord will save me." The three men in the rubber raft went on to save others in need.

The deluge of rain continued and the river rose even higher. The man climbed to the top of his chimney. One foot on each side of the flue, he shouted at the rain, his fist held defiantly in the air. At this point, a helicopter with a ladder arrived. The men inside yelled to the man on the roof, "Grab the ladder and we will take you to safety." Again the man declined the offer. He waved them off, shouting to them, "The Lord will save me!" The helicopter departed to rescue others.

With a flash of light the man on the roof suddenly found himself at the pearly gates. The Lord greeted him and welcomed him to his kingdom.

The man, now confused, asked the Lord, "Why didn't you save me?" He paused and added, "I believed you would save me and yet I ended up here."

The Lord replied, "I'm so sorry, sir. I sent two boats and a helicopter. I didn't know what else to do."

The man on the roof had a plan. It just wasn't the right plan. . . .

Do not let this happen to you.

INTRODUCTION

Life, so amazing and so unpredictable. We greet each morning with great expectations, only to have the reality of life interrupt our plans. How do we expect the best, yet prepare for the unexpected? How do we avoid obsessing about everything that can go wrong and the paralysis this approach creates? Ignorance is not bliss. You cannot be an ostrich and come through life's disasters well.

Disasters are detours in life's journey. Because disasters exist, we can recognize a perfect day. Disasters are the counter-point that reminds us of what real joy feels like. They **DO** make us stronger. They improve our coping and problem-solving skills. Most importantly, you cannot avoid them so you must be prepared to face them. Only then will you be in charge of your recovery and be able to move forward in a meaningful way.

Disasters have many faces. Major natural disasters affect thousands to millions of people every year. Health issues, minor and major, affect not only an individual but the entire family. Accidents, big and small, occur when we are least prepared for them. Divorce or the death of a spouse or parent creates numerous personal disasters that can be overwhelming for the one left behind. Small disasters, from flat tires to running toilets, interrupt life at inopportune times, causing chaos.

Planning for the unexpected is the fuel for many professions. Financial advisors hope to guide you through the labyrinth of investments so that you can retire comfortably. Lawyers specialize in estate planning and other legal documents. Insurance agents present numerous options to protect your possessions, your health, and your family. These are all important pieces of the plan. They can be disjointed elements or part of an integrated plan that can help you navigate through life's bumps and bruises.

This book provides a guide to help you prepare for disasters. You will identify and collect your resources, securely store important documents, and create a roadmap for you and family members to find important information to get beyond any disaster. Knowledge replaces helplessness and presents formidable empowerment for the most positive outcome possible. While it may be impossible to avoid life's disasters, it is very possible to minimize the impact the disaster has on our life.

Shit happens!

TABLE OF CONTENTS

xvi

1   SHIT DEFINED

What exactly am I speaking about when I say "Shit Happens"?

For the purposes of this book "shit" is defined as the unexpected life events that disrupt and cause chaos in our lives. They are the things that we worry about often. The things that keep us up at night. The "what ifs" that can paralyze us with fear and a feeling of helplessness.

There are many "what ifs" when it comes to natural disasters.

What if the wildfire coming over the hill takes my home in the conflagration? What if the hurricane a thousand miles away makes a beeline for my area? What if the tornado siren goes off in the middle of the night? What if the raising river floods me out? What if there is an earthquake, flash flood, house fire, train derailment, sink hole, the dam fails, or an act of war that forces me from my home?

These events can often force you to leave your home on short notice. It could be days, hours, or minutes before you have to get out.

Would you be able to get everything you need together in time?
Do you know where your important papers are?
Your treasured photographs?
Insurance documents?
Financial papers?
Do you have a TO-GO bag?
Does your family know where to meet up?

There are just as many "what ifs" when unexpected life changes occur.

What if I get really sick?
What if my spouse or child becomes seriously ill?
How can I help my aging parents prepare?
What if my marriage ends in divorce?
What if my spouse suddenly dies?
What if I am deployed with the military and have to leave my family for a prolonged period of time?
What if I become disabled?

How would you manage the financial responsibility you suddenly must undertake if you find yourself alone? Would you know where the investments are? The insurance policies? Legal documents? How to pay the bills? Online passwords? Would you know when to turn off the sprinkler system or how to close the pool? Would you know how to operate the coffee pot, vacuum cleaner, or the washing machine if you had never done so?

How would you deal with the emotional healing process when you are so overwhelmed with just surviving? The upheaval in dealing with aspects of life you may have never been involved with before can leave you feeling like you are drowning.

A long list of little things can go wrong that can throw your life into turmoil.

What if the car breaks down, you have an accident, or you get a flat tire? Would you know what to do? Would you know who to call? Do you know if you can trust the repair-person?

A thousand things can happen if you are a homeowner. What if your toilet runs, causing your septic system to back up into the basement? What if a pipe freezes while you are away during a power outage? What if that frozen pipe bursts and you have a major flood when you return? Would you know what to do if your washing machine hose suddenly springs a leak? You smell gas? Your roof starts leaking? Your bathtub drain is slow? You get a shock from an electrical appliance or outlet? What if your home is robbed?

This all may sound like a lot of doom and gloom. But I know these are the things we all worry about. I know because I have worried about them too. We all know people who have faced one or more of these issues. You may have already come face-to-face with similar disasters yourself. That's what validates our worry in the first place. Often bad things pile one on top of another, causing life to spin out of control.

This can leave you feeling frustrated, helpless, and angry.

How do you move forward from there?

2   WHEN THE SHIT HITS THE FAN

Have you ever had one of those days? A day when everything seems to go wrong?

You don't know why, but no matter what you do you can't get things back together.

That sounds pretty bad doesn't it?

Now imagine the worst day of your life. . . .
A natural disaster just destroyed your home.
Your spouse dies suddenly.

That truly is a day when everything did go wrong. You can't see how your life can ever be put back together. What can you do to recover from something so overwhelming?

The impact is bigger than anything you can imagine. It feels like you are sinking in quicksand and you cannot move your arms and legs.

You can't breathe. You feel so lost, afraid, confused, stupid, and angry. "How can this happen to me?" you ask.

"What do I do now?"

"Who do I call?"

"Where do I even begin?"

Friends and family may or may not offer to help you. Some of the help will be truly beneficial. Some of that help may be misguided and just plain wrong.

Some people will offer help that only serves their own interests and will not serve you. How can you know if it is good help or bad?

When you are in such an emotionally fragile state, you may not be able to make the best decisions for your future. You may be tempted to allow others to make decisions for you because you have been paralyzed by the disaster you are facing. This is not a good place to be.

Avoid making any big decisions until you have had time to think about them clearly. Decisions made in haste or based on fear may not serve your best interest in the long run.

Disasters can strike at any time. How you prepare for them determines how you survive them. Worry will never solve anything. You must have a plan.

You must believe that only good things will happen yet be prepared for the worst. Only then will you have the peace of mind that comes with knowing you have prepared for your future, no matter what happens.

Your plan will help you make the right decisions because you have thought things through before a disaster happens. You have created a plan with a clear head, without the emotional baggage that a disaster brings to the table or when you are in the middle of it.

It is like wearing a raincoat when the shit hits the fan. There **IS** going to be a mess to clean up, but you will come out of it wearing the least amount of that mess . . .

. . . if you are prepared.

3 MURPHY'S LAW: IF ANYTHING CAN GO WRONG IT WILL

Shit happens to everyone.

Picture this: Everything in your life is humming along like a well-oiled machine. You are happy. Life is good. You are thinking about what you are going to do this day, your job, your children, what you are having for dinner.

Then suddenly, you hear water running. At first you are not concerned. Maybe someone flushed the toilet or is washing a dish. You listen for it to stop. It does not. You search the house for the source. You open the basement door. The noise is louder. You flip on the light and go down the stairs. Then you see it. Water cascades from the pipe by the boiler. An inch of water is already on the floor.

What you do next can limit the damage or it can make things worse.

Do you know what to do?

Do you scream helplessly, "OMG, there is a flood"?

Do you go back upstairs, close the door, and call the plumber?

Do you grab the mop?

Do you start picking up things in danger of getting wet?

Do you call the insurance agent?

First things first.

TURN THE WATER OFF to stop the flooding.
How do you do that?
Do you know where the water shut off is?

Shit happens every day.
That is just one of the truths of life.
You can go with the flow, deal with it, and laugh about it later, or you can allow yourself to be a victim and cry and whine about it. The choice is yours.

Knowing how to deal with the things that happen every day is empowering.

I want everyone reading this book to feel empowered. You do not have to be devastated by the bumps in the road that everyone faces.

When you look at others, do you see them as having a perfect life, where nothing ever goes wrong? That is probably not reality. They have as many obstacles as you. They just handle them differently.

The bumps in the road are the things that make life interesting. They help us become better people. They make us stronger. They can make us laugh and they can make us cry.

While Murphy's Law says if anything can go wrong it will, do not allow it to suck you into pessimism and despair. Know that **YOU** have within you the power to overcome whatever adversity that life throws in your path. Approach life's disasters in a positive way, with solutions, and you can appear to have a perfect life too.

4 IT'S NOT NICE TO FOOL MOTHER NATURE

No matter where you live, you are vulnerable to natural disasters.

Mother Nature does not discriminate. Rich or poor, happy, sad, prepared or not, there is nothing you can do to avoid the disaster if you happen to be in the target zone.

We see it on television and read about it every day; somewhere, a disaster is striking someone. We breathe a sigh of relief when it is not us. But, in our hearts, we know that something similar could happen to us at any time.

I would like to address some specific threats from Mother Nature.

WILDFIRE

Fires burn thousands of acres every year in the United States. There are droughts that effect different regions of the country for short or long periods of time. Drought combined with wind conditions and natural or man-made ignition can start a wildfire.

Wildfires were a natural part of nature's renewal process prior to man developing the land. America's heartland, the great prairie, was largely devoid of trees because the prairies would burn every year. Fires triggered by lightning strikes would consume tens of thousands of acres.

The pine barrens of Long Island and New Jersey were also prone to fires. In fact, the fires produced the heat necessary for the scrub pine cones to open and release their seeds.

The giant redwoods in California record a history of fires in their growth rings. Bruised, but not destroyed, they have stood for hundreds of years.

Unfortunately, our homes may not fare as well. We have all seen the charred remains of once beautiful homes reduced to foundation and chimney, the contents scorched, melted, and unrecognizable.

Picture this: you awake in the morning to the smell of smoke hanging heavy in the air. You have heard the fire trucks throughout the night. The fire in the next canyon seems remote. While you are concerned, you watch somewhat detached.

The flames suddenly appear at the top of the hill. Police cars roll down the street. Officers knocking on every door inform you and your neighbors that you must evacuate NOW. There is no time to waste. Get out now, don't look back. Don't hesitate. You must save yourself and your family.

What do you manage to bring with you?
When you are able to come back, will your home still be there?
What do you do now?

Where do you begin?

If you live in a fire-prone area you may have thought about a plan. Maybe you have been evacuated before and been lucky because the fire missed you. Thinking about a plan and actually having a plan are two different things. Protecting yourself and your family should be your top priority. The only way to do this is with a real, concrete plan.

TORNADO

In the spring and fall, large disparate air masses collide in America's heartland, creating ideal conditions for tornados. Long lines of thunderstorms march across the countryside with great potential of spinning off tornados at any moment.

All eyes watch the looming storm clouds, looking for telltale signs. The National Weather Service issues watches and warnings. A warning is only posted once a tornado is on the ground. Even then, there is difficulty in predicting where it will go next and how big or intense it will be.

If your home is in the path of the tornado, there is sure to be significant damage, if not complete destruction. There are few things as frightening as a tornado. It is the monster of our nightmares.

Envision this: It is a beautiful spring day, unusually warm. The sky is blue, but the weatherman says that there is a chance of strong thunderstorms later in the afternoon. Evening comes and the sky remains clear. The weatherman is still predicting stormy weather. You have heard it a million times before. The storms must be somewhere, but not here. You tuck your children in for the night and go to bed.

You are startled awake by the tornado sirens. There is an ominous wind. The storm is already here. You have minutes to get into your tornado shelter, if you have one. If you don't, you gather the children and head into the basement. You huddle next to the foundation, pull an old mattress over your heads, hold on for dear life, and pray.

The sound of the storm is deafening. You hear your home being blown apart above you. It is over in a flash. Everyone is all right, frightened, but okay. The silence is punctuated by crying, moaning, police and fire sirens.

You emerge from the basement to survey the damage.

Nothing is left.

Now what?

HURRICANE

Hurricane season in the US is from June to November. While hurricanes are tropical in origin, they are able to cover great distances. Hurricanes produce numerous potential damaging forces. We most often think of wind damage with hurricanes. But as we saw with Katrina, Irene, and Sandy, the storm surge and the heavy rains were what produced the greatest devastation.

The gulf coast of Mississippi saw a wall of water from Katrina's storm surge that reached miles inland. It destroyed everything in its path. It leveled buildings and deposited large boats far from the water. The heavy rains caused the levy breaches in New Orleans, leaving the South Ward under water and many dead.

The torrential rains from Irene, which was downgraded from a hurricane to a tropical storm as it marched inland across upstate New York and Vermont, caused usually placid creeks and streams to overflow their banks, scouring new paths in a thousand-year flood. In Vermont, treasured covered bridges were destroyed by the powerful flow of water. Entire towns were inundated, and road access was cut off for weeks. These areas had never seen flooding like this before.

In 2012, Superstorm Sandy marched up the east coast, delivering its dual blow of catastrophic coastal flooding in New York City and Long Island, along with strong winds that toppled trees and turned the electrical grid into spaghetti. Many were without power for weeks and many still struggle to rebuild their homes and lives more than two years after.

Hurricanes are slow-moving. We often have several days to prepare for their arrival. When evacuations are ordered, many people leave. There are always those who don't or won't, and those who delay their departure until it is too late. When it is too late, you have no choice but to hunker down and pray.

Usually you have enough time to put together important papers, treasured photographs, and things you can pack in your car.

> Would you know what to pack?
> What do you need to bring with you?
> Do you have a checklist?

FLOODS

Every year, numerous flooding events occur along rivers great and small. The spring snowmelt and/or heavy rains put more water into the river system than the riverbanks can control.

Historically, the annual river flooding was the source of the abundance of fertile soil found in the river valleys. It was this fertile soil that attracted man to settle in these valleys and cultivate their crops. The very thing that made the valleys attractive to settlers also put them in danger. Annual floodwaters could carry away everything man had built, and often did.

Over time, we learned to tame these rivers. We built dams and carefully controlled the flow of water. We were able to stop the annual flooding along the Tennessee River.

On other rivers, the dams and levees were able to control flooding downstream but, at the same time, created new flooding upstream. It is simple math;

when the volume of water exceeds the volume the riverbanks can hold, the water spills out onto the surrounding flood plain. It is called a **FLOODPLAIN** and therein lies the clue that you are in danger if and when the river floods.

Floods can be particularly devastating, not only in their destructive power, but also from the potential contamination by toxins and disease that flooding often brings. Rebuilding after a flood comes with its own special challenges.

Did you assemble the important papers you needed beforehand?
Is that moldy, wadded up pile of glop in the corner what is left of your insurance policy?
Homeowners insurance does not cover flooding.
Did you have flood insurance?
Were you current on your premiums?
Were you past the mandatory waiting period prior to your loss?

EARTHQUAKE

Earthquakes are not just a concern for those in California. There are many high risk earthquake zones in the US. Alaska, Hawaii, Memphis, St Louis, New York, and even Washington, DC, are in the crosshairs of a major earthquake.

Earthquakes pose many dangers, including building, road, and bridge collapse. There is the potential for widespread disruption of water, gas, and electric supply. The risk of fire from ruptured gas lines is real. Firestorms can ignite in areas dominated by wooden structures. As we saw recently in Japan and Thailand, there is also the risk of tsunami.

Earthquakes can be accompanied by volcanic eruptions, which come with their own list of potential catastrophes. These include mudslides, lava, pyroclastic flow, ash clouds, and toxic gases.

Predicting earthquakes is an inexact science. The scientists may know that the earth is building up to something but, they cannot say exactly when or how strong it will be.

Your best defense is to be prepared.

What does that preparation look like?

BLIZZARDS AND ICE STORMS

Every year, large swaths of the country are covered with snow and ice. Smaller storms are an inconvenience and part of living in the northern parts of the US and higher elevations. Blizzards, however, pose significant problems and dangers and ice storms can be even more deadly.

Both have the potential to strand you in your home for days. You could be stranded in your vehicle with no help in sight. Power outages can cause life-threatening problems. The extreme cold conditions during and following these storms can exacerbate the problem. Downed power lines from heavy ice loads and falling trees can make getting around impossible and dangerous. Roads can be impassable as clearing them can take days. Heavy snow and/or ice loads can cause roofs and buildings to collapse.

Recent ice storms in the south presented special problems as communities lacked the equipment to effectively deal with a relatively small amount of snow and ice, leaving people stranded for nearly a week. But, even when a community has the equipment and knows how to deal with these storms, sometimes Mother Nature really slams it with something they never expected, e.g., the Montreal Ice Storm that left a coating of ice several inches thick on everything, and left thousands of people without power for weeks in the middle of winter.

The good news is that we usually have some notice that a blizzard or ice storm is coming. That means that we can shop for necessities beforehand. This puts a lot of stress on local food distribution, making it difficult to refill barren shelves immediately afterwards. If you do not shop before the storm, it may be difficult to find the things you need after the storm is over.

The real dangers from these storms occur when the power is off for a significant length of time. When people are trapped in their homes, there is a strong possibility of hypothermia as the house gets colder and colder. Using high risk, alternative heat sources such as kerosene heaters can produce dangerous levels of carbon monoxide and be a fire hazard. You

21

should never use a gas oven to heat the house. Consider investing in a generator but make sure that you never run it inside the house.

How well are you prepared for a blizzard or ice storm?

OTHER NATURAL AND MAN-MADE DISASTERS

There is a long list of other natural and man-made disasters. They can affect individuals, small groups of people, or entire towns.

This includes sinkholes, house fires, train derailments, plane crashes, toxic spills, home or factory explosions, underground chemical plumes, structure failure, hail storm damage, wind damage, mudslides, rockslides, avalanche, extreme drought, nuclear leaks, water main breaks, and gas line ruptures. Finally, let's not forget the disasters of acts of war, terror attacks, and riots. I am sure there are others not listed here that you have heard about or experienced yourself.

Any one of these things can force evacuation from your home with or without warning.

Once again, if you are prepared, you can get through whatever you must with the least amount of pain.

Spending time worrying is wasted time. If you lie awake at night thinking about these things, you will only lose sleep and make yourself sick in the process.

22

What are you going to do to protect your family?

Are you willing to do the necessary preparation?

Now let's see what planning looks like.

POINTS TO PONDER

NATURAL DISASTERS

Your vulnerability to specific natural disasters varies by your geography.

What natural disasters are you likely to experience? These are the things that require your attention and planning.

- Wildfire
- Tornado
- Hurricane
- Earthquake
- Tsunami
- Volcanic eruption
- Flood
- Blizzard
- Ice Storm
- Sinkhole
- Hailstorm
- Mudslide
- Rockslide
- Avalanche

Which natural disasters do you need to prepare for?

Just because it has not happened before or has not happened in many years does not mean it cannot happen.

MAN-MADE DISASTERS

What is your risk of experiencing a man-made disaster?

Many of these show up in the environment and may put your family at risk. Evaluate your risk for these disasters based on proximity to your home.

- Train derailment
- Plane crashes
- Dam failure
- Water main break
- Toxic spills
- Underground chemical plumes
- House fires
- Factory explosions
- Gas line explosions
- Acts of war
- Terrorism
- Riots

Points to Ponder (continued)

The need for **evacuation** due to a man-made disaster is often presented without warning. How well you are prepared will impact your recovery.

5   PREPARING FOR NATURAL DISASTERS

Where do I begin?
It all starts with the big picture.

Your big picture plan must include a number of pieces. For your plan to be viable, you should make your plan well in advance of needing it. Communicate your plan with all family members to insure that each family member knows what to do in case of an emergency.

CREATING YOUR EMERGENCY PLAN

Assemble and secure your important documents.

Have insurance and legal documents in place.

Set up an ICE (in case of emergency) contact list and physical and/or computer file.

Establish a meet-up location you can use if your family members become separated.

Create a checklist for emergencies.

Address what to do with pets during and after the emergency

Assemble your family emergency kit. Your emergency kit should be inspected every three to six months to make sure that batteries and foodstuffs are not outdated and that clothing is properly sized for growing children.

Finally, share the plan with family members.

If you do all these things, you will be able to weather whatever Mother Nature throws at you. You may already have a number of the things on this list done.

ADVANCE PLANNING

You probably already have homeowner's or renter's insurance.

You may be surprised to find out you live in a flood zone. Your homeowner's insurance does not cover flood damage. Federal flood insurance is the only way to be covered for floods. There is a waiting period for the coverage to be in force, usually six months. This is another reason to plan ahead.

Also be aware of important deductibles in your homeowner's insurance policies for wind damage. Know what natural disasters you are at risk for. Have a conversation with your insurance agent to make sure you have the proper coverage. This is an essential part of disaster planning.

Legal preparation should also be part of your disaster plan. Wills, trusts, living wills, powers of attorney, and healthcare proxies should be in place. Consult with a legal professional to put these essential documents in place.

CREATING YOUR "ICE" (IN CASE OF EMERGENCY) FILE

Assembling your important documents is the next step. Birth certificates, baptismal certificates, marriage license, divorce decree, deed for the house, certificate of occupancy, property survey, mortgage papers, loan documents, homeowner's insurance policy, mortgage insurance policy, car insurance policies, health insurance, umbrella policy, long-term care policies, life insurance policies, disability policies, stock certificates and other financial information, such as bank account information, investment accounts, broker contacts, as well as legal documents such as wills, trusts, healthcare proxy, living wills, powers of attorney, passports and passport numbers, copies of drivers licenses and health insurance cards, copies or lists of credit card numbers. Be sure to include pet vaccination, ID chip, and licensing information.

Keep **three sets** of these documents.
1. Put one copy in a fireproof safe in your home.
2. The original copies should be kept in a safe deposit box in a bank of your choosing.
3. Finally, an electronic copy should be stored in a secure vault in the cloud.

If you do this, you will be assured that at least one copy will survive in case of a disaster. If your home is destroyed, you could access your documents in the safe deposit box. If the community is destroyed, you will still have cloud access. If the internet is gone, you will have access to one of the two hard copies. If all three are gone, you probably will not need them anyway.

ICE (In Case of Emergency)

Create an emergency contact list on your phone. Emergency personnel are trained to look in cell phones for ICE contacts. I enter my ICE contacts this way:

First Name: ICE (contact name)
Last Name: (relationship)
Phone: ### ### ####
Cell Phone: ###-###-####

Create an emergency instruction page on your computer. This will also be labeled ICE (in case of emergency). This will help your family know what your wishes are and help them access your information if they need to. Make sure you have a password keeper program that will help gain access to your vault and other computer-maintained accounts. I would maintain that password keeper separate from your vault in the cloud for security purposes. If you do not have a computer, a file folder labeled ICE is an effective alternative.

WHERE TO MEET UP

Your emergency plan must include a meeting location outside of the home where family members will meet. During a natural disaster, cell service is often disrupted. You cannot count on your cell phones to keep you connected. You may want to set up several options.

Plan A may be across the street three doors down, for a local event affecting only your home.

Plan B may be the police station, fire station, hospital, or Red Cross tent. These locations assemble the names of those looking for others. They will keep you safe until you are reunited with your loved ones. Small children who become separated from their families should approach the first emergency person they see. It is important to have some type of identification affixed to your child with name, birth date, address, parents' names, and cell phone numbers. This will help identify and reunite your family as quickly as possible. In fact, all family members should have identification with them.

CREATE YOUR PERSONAL CHECKLIST

What are the things you need in an emergency that are not practical to pack in advance? They are the things that are essential for your health and well-being. They may be the things you use every day or they may be things for which you are unlikely to have duplicates. Your pocketbook, wallet, cell phone, medication, walker, wheelchair, cane, supplements, oxygen generator, insulin pump, breast pump, car seat, dentures, contacts, glasses, sturdy shoes, GPS, and the like.

These are the things you may forget in the panic of the moment. Creating a checklist that you can use if you have to leave your home will help you avoid serious problems.

Other things to put on the checklist may include family photographs, treasured heirlooms, jewelry, and collectables.

Do not forget CASH. Since there could be electrical disruption during the emergency, you may not have access to a cash machine or be able to use credit cards.

Do not forget your pets! Take them with you if you can. Leaving them behind creates another type of disaster later. They may perish, escape, become lost, injured, or otherwise traumatized. Have a carrier for each dog or cat. Have leashes and food bowls, extra water, and food supplies. Shelters may require proof of immunizations. This should be part of your emergency kit.

A full tank of gas is a critical. You want to be able to drive as far as you can from the disaster area. If there is a significant disruption to the electrical grid, finding gas afterwards may be difficult.

PREASSEMBLE YOUR FAMILY EMERGENCY KIT

The family emergency kit contains all the essential items you need to survive for a minimum of three to seven days post-disaster.

Preparing your kit begins with creating a checklist for it. You will be able to put together a number of things well in advance of an emergency: flashlights, batteries, rope, duct tape, radio, multi-blade knife, waterproof matches, can opener, blankets or sleeping bags, pillows, one or two changes of clothes, underwear, jacket, sweatshirt, socks, soap, toothpaste, toothbrushes, toiletries, feminine hygiene products, washcloth, towels, diapers, water (one-half gallon per person per day), canned tuna, canned chicken, peanut butter, jelly, crackers, canned soup, juice boxes, hard candy, evaporated milk, cereal, coffee, teabags, large pot for boiling water, paper plates and cups, plastic utensils, paper towels, toilet paper, hand sanitizer, water purifier tablets, tarp, camp chairs, plastic garbage bags, playing cards, a rubber ball, stuffed toy, and other non-electronic entertainment for the kids.

Keep the list of personal items that cannot be pre-packed taped to the top of your emergency kit. Make sure you add those important things, checked off one at a time and added to your kit before you leave the house.

Pack your emergency kit in a large plastic tote that can be easily transported. Mark it clearly. Keep the checklist taped to the top. Inspect your emergency kit every three months to insure you have no expired products and that batteries are fresh. You can break your kit up into two totes: one for food and one for non-perishables

You should also have a cooler as part of your emergency kit. This will allow you to bring a small amount of perishables with you if you are evacuated. . Consider keeping two quart jugs of water in the freezer at all times, pre-frozen so they are ready when you need to keep perishables cold. As they defrost, you can drink them, so they do double duty.

You can download your free Disaster Planning Checklist at: www.TheCrisisPlanner.com.

Additional sources for an Emergency Kit Checklist:

- Federal Emergency Management Agency (FEMA)
- State and Local Governments
- Red Cross
- Emergency preparation websites
- Medicare – for kidney dialysis patients and other health issues

Customize your checklist and emergency kit for your family needs.

Now you are prepared for any natural disaster that Mother Nature will throw at you.
What is the worst-case scenario?

Your home is totally destroyed and you have to start over.

With a proper plan in place, you will know that you have done everything you can to get on with life afterwards.

Let us discuss situations you may face before, during, and after a natural disaster.

EVACUATION

You are being told to evacuate before a disaster.

You have several options to consider. Can you travel out of the danger zone before the disaster strikes?

Do you have family or friends outside the danger zone who are willing to house you and your family until you can return to your home?

Can you find hotel/motel accommodations outside the danger zone? Call ahead and guarantee your reservation if you plan to use a hotel/motel.

Where is the shelter that can accommodate your needs for family and pets? Get there early so you do not get shut out.

Once you choose your option, it is time to pull out the checklist and pack the car. Do not wait until the last minute. It is always better to err on the side of caution when it comes to your family's safety. If evacuation involves a large number of people, roadways will become clogged with those leaving the area, making the trip longer than anticipated.

Turn off the water, gas, and pull the main breaker. This will reduce the risk of fire, and flooding during your absence. You may lose food in your refrigerator and freezer but that is a small price to pay if you ultimately reduce damage to your home.

Run through your checklist to make sure you have everything and everyone on it. Check your list twice. You will not be back until the danger is past. You will be unable to run out to the store for forgotten items. What you pack is what you have.

Remember, space will be at a premium in the car, hotel room, family or friend's house, or the shelter. It is guaranteed to be crowded, noisy, and uncomfortable. It is not going to feel like home. Your proper preparation will make it as comfortable as possible.

Most importantly, pack a positive attitude, patience, and your smile. These things will help you through anything.

STAYING IN YOUR HOME

What if you are weathering a natural disaster in your home?

What if you are not evacuated for a hurricane, blizzard, or ice-storm?

What if the power goes out and you are trapped in your home? What if the roads are impassable? What if there are downed wires everywhere?

What if the phone is out, cell service is spotty, and cable and internet are down?

It is time to stay safe and hunker down.

IMPORTANT - If you have a medical issue that requires power twenty-four hours a day, it is important that you notify local emergency services prior to the storm so they can assist you.

Loss of power can create a life-threatening situation and alternative power options must be in place. This may require that the person be relocated to a hospital setting prior to the storm to keep them safe.

If there is a possibility that power will be lost, it is a good idea to have a portable generator. I recommend testing your generator before the power goes out to make sure you know how to operate it and that it is running properly. Do this at the beginning of hurricane season or in the fall before winter storms are a threat. Making repairs when there is not an emergency is a wise move. Buying a generator before there is a threat of a storm will save you money and time as there is always a shortage immediately before and during the disaster. Where there is scarcity, there is price gouging.

Most portable generators are designed for limited emergency power. They can run your refrigerator, freezer, a television, a couple of lights, and a radio for several hours at a time.

You do not need to run your generator more than three or four times a day to keep your food safe. This will conserve your gasoline consumption and give you a break from the noise. It will allow you to watch a movie on DVD while it is running, and charge cell phones, your computer, and other rechargeable electronic devices.

Fuel for your generator will go quickly. Make sure you have portable gas cans filled in advance of any storm. Your car should also have a full tank of gas. Trying to find gasoline after a storm can become a challenge if the power outage is widespread. Long gas lines after Sandy created tension and frustration as people waited for hours trying to fill gas cans and vehicles.

You can simplify the set up for a portable generator by having electrical work done in advance that will isolate specific circuits, allowing for easy plug in of the generator.

If you are in a high risk area for these storms and experience frequent, long power outages you may want to invest in a whole house generator system. This represents a significant investment. But it can give you total peace of mind that you will be fully functioning during the outage.

During a power outage, your charcoal or gas grill can be your best friend. You can cook almost anything on one of them. You can even boil water to wash the dishes and for bathing. Make sure you have enough charcoal and lighter fluid or gas for the grill to get you through. Never use a charcoal or gas grill inside the house. They produce carbon-monoxide gas which is very dangerous.

Avoid using candles to light your home. They present a high risk of fire. Use battery-powered lanterns and flashlights. The new LED flashlights create a brighter light and have long battery life. It is important to have replacement batteries. There are many solar lanterns on the market. You can find them online and they are easy to pack in your emergency kit. Rechargeable lights are another option. Remember to recharge them when your generator is running.

Keeping the house warm can be a challenge. You may have an alternate heat source, a wood or coal stove or fireplace. If you use this for your primary heat source, you will burn a lot more wood or coal than usual. Make sure you have easy access to your fuel.

Never use a stove or oven to heat your home. Kerosene heaters pose a high risk of carbon-monoxide poisoning. They should be used only where there is adequate ventilation.

Your choice of clothing is also important. Cotton is a poor choice for warmth. Wool insulates best and allows moisture to wick away from your skin, keeping you warmer. Layer clothing as necessary to keep warm. Pay close attention to small children as they can lose body heat quickly and are more vulnerable to hypothermia. Sleeping in the room with the heat source will be more comfortable. Sleeping bags are designed to keep body heat in when outside temperatures are very cold. Hats, gloves, and scarves will also keep you warm and safe.

If it is very cold, you have a high risk of freezing pipes. High winds with very cold temperatures increase that risk. If you have a forced hot air heating system, your risk is lower. But pipes in the kitchen and bathroom may still freeze. If the temperature in the house drops below forty-five degrees, allow the water to drip freely from the faucet. This will keep the water moving and prevent freezing.

If you have baseboard heating, your risk can be significant. Pipes in overhangs are particularly vulnerable to freezing. If you have electrical work done to facilitate a portable generator, I recommend putting your circulator and heating plant on that line. Even if you are running your portable generator only three or four times a day, it will heat and circulate the water in the pipes and prevent freezing.

Frozen pipes can make things even more difficult. You may not know that pipes are frozen until the power is back on. The process of freezing stops the flow of water. When the house warms up and the water in the pipes melts, the floodgates may open.

If you have any fear that your pipes may be frozen, stay in your home during the warming process to insure there is no break in the system. If they have burst, there will be a flood. During the warming process, if you hear water running or see a leak anywhere in the system, turn off the main water valve to minimize the damage and call the plumber.

Be aware that emergency services may be in your community to distribute water and other necessities. Do not be afraid to ask what, when, and where they will be.

Reach out to elderly neighbors who also may be stranded. Check on them to make sure they are safe and have access to essential supplies. If you believe them to be in danger, contact your local emergency services to have them looked after.

Your attitude will determine how you get through the crisis. If you remain positive and upbeat, make it an adventure and fun for the kids, it will be merely an inconvenience. You will be able to laugh about it and it may even bring your family closer together.

YOU ARE STRANDED IN YOUR CAR

We spend a great deal of time in our cars. Sometimes we make choices that put us in danger. We go out on a snowy day or in a heavy downpour. The pavement may be icy, dry, or wet. Accidents happen, cars break down, or you end up in a ditch or a snow bank. You become stranded on a desolate stretch of road with no one in sight. You are stuck in your car. This is another case in which you can prepare for disaster and survive.

Your car emergency kit is essential. What should be in your car? There are many prepackaged automobile emergency kits. They include things like jumper cables, hazard triangles, flares, a mini first-aid kit, and a HELP sign. Other important things you should have include protein bars, water, hard candy, a space blanket, a multi-tool, a phone charger, a seat-belt cutter. An inflatable emergency sausage is available that hangs out the window and is eight to ten feet tall. Its bright coloring is easy to see and may help rescuers find you in a blizzard.

Winter driving conditions can change quickly. Preparation before you leave the house is more important in the winter because the risk is higher. Fill your gas tank. Check your tire pressure, antifreeze, oil, and windshield washer fluid levels. Change your windshield wipers as necessary. Consider getting snow blades that do not get iced up in a snow storm. Make sure your defroster, front and rear, and your heater are operating correctly.

Carry an ice scrapper, shovel, kitty litter or sand, ice grippers, hat, gloves, scarf, and warm coat. Many of us do not drive wearing all these clothes, but if you are stuck, you will be very happy to have them with you. In some states and locations, snow tires or chains may be required under certain driving conditions. Have your ICE (in case of emergency) contacts labeled clearly in your cell phone. Wear a medical alert bracelet or pendent that will inform rescue personnel of any medical conditions you have.

Black Ice is a real hazard that is totally unpredictable. You often cannot see it. You do not know it is there until you are skidding uncontrollably. If you are alone on the road and skid off into the trees, it may be a long time before someone finds you, especially if you are injured or unconscious. The risk of chain reaction accidents is high as cars and trucks pile into one another on the ice. It is recommended that you stay in your car as long as it is safe. Walking around in these conditions may put you a higher risk of injury or death with multiple vehicles careening out of control. Your body is no match for a five thousand pound vehicle impacting you at high speed.

- Snowy, icy, or wet roads present many hazards. Use caution when you drive in those conditions.
- Reduce your speed, allow more space between vehicles, and anticipate what other drivers are going to do and mistakes they could make.
- Be attentive to driving.
- Don't text and drive. If you must use your cell phone while driving, use it hands-free.

Expect to arrive at your destination safely, yet be prepared for whatever disaster can happen.

YOUR HOME IS DESTROYED IN THE DISASTER

Sometimes things happen so quickly you do not have the opportunity to get to your emergency checklist or emergency kit, such as a house fire, tornado, chemical spill, train derailment, or earthquake that renders your home uninhabitable.

Sometimes you evacuate your home and it is destroyed in your absence by water, wind, or fire.

In either case, if your disaster plan is in place, all of your important documents will still be safe. This will allow you to contact insurance agents and start the claim and rebuilding process. You will have everything you need to start over.

The Red Cross and other emergency services can arrange temporary housing until you or your insurance agent can get something more permanent while your home is being rebuilt or restored.

This is a time when patience is essential. Do not, however, be passive. Squeaky wheels do get greased. There may be many people with claims and that can slow the process.

You may have lost your home and everything in it, but, those are things. Things can be replaced. It is time to take care of the injured and bury the dead as necessary. It is time to get on with living. The disaster cannot take your memories for they are in your mind and heart forever.

Natural disasters are unpredictable and pose real danger to you and your family. Preparation does not make you paranoid. You are dealing with the reality of living in a constructive way by being prepared. Once you are prepared, you can let the worry go. Worry is destructive and a waste of your time.

Planning and preparation are liberating. You are freed to live life fully, knowing you are prepared for anything that can go wrong.

Proper preparation will help you recover faster.

Preparation will allow you and your family to move forward with life.

PLANNING PEARLS

"ICE" (In Case of Emergency)

- Set up ICE contacts in your cell phone.
- Set up an "ICE" file on your computer.
- Set up an "ICE" folder in your file cabinet or safe.

DOCUMENT STORAGE – THREE LOCATIONS

- Fireproof safe at home
- Safe-deposit box at your bank
- Secure vault in the cloud

YOUR EMERGENCY KIT

- Things you can pack in advance. Re-check often to insure batteries are fresh, no foodstuffs are outdated, and the clothing still fits growing children.
- Things you must pack in the event of an emergency that you use every day. Make a list of these things and tape it on top of your pre-packed emergency kit.
- Download your free Disaster Planning Checklist at: www.TheCrisisPlanner.com

Planning Pearls (continued)

- Additional sources for Emergency Kit Checklists are: Red Cross, the FEMA, state and local websites, and Medicare for specific medical conditions such as kidney failure.

PLAN YOUR EMERGENCY EVACUATION

- Avoid the crush, leave as early as possible.
- Make arrangements for hotel/motel in advance.
- Take your pets with you, bring proof of vaccination.
- Notify family and friends that you are leaving the danger area.

PLAN HOW TO KEEP YOUR FAMILY SAFE IF YOU STAY IN YOUR HOME

- Fill your car's gas tank.
- Pre-test your generator and have enough fuel.
- Avoid candles, kerosene heaters, and do not use the oven to heat your home.
- Protect pipes from freezing in winter by allowing faucets to drip if power is out.
- Do not use a charcoal or gas grills indoors.

Planning Pearls (continued)

- Do use a gas or charcoal grill outdoors for cooking and hot water needs.

PLAN HOW TO KEEP YOURSELF SAFE IF YOU BECOME STRANDED IN YOUR CAR

- Make sure your car is maintained. Check tires, oil, antifreeze, and windshield washer fluid levels. Replace windshield wipers, and pack a complete emergency kit.
- Avoid driving in hazardous conditions if you can. Drive smarter and slower as per road conditions.

PLAN WHAT TO DO IF YOUR HOME IS DESTROYED IN A DISASTER

- Rebuild from the ashes . . . armed with your essential documents
- Keep a positive attitude, be patient, and smile.
- Take it one day at a time.
- Be grateful to be alive.

6   AS LONG AS YOU HAVE YOUR HEALTH

Health is something many of us take for granted, until you face a health crisis.

The health of your spouse, children, parent, or yourself can create significant stress in the household. A health crisis can be a result of an accident or from an illness.

Health issues often come on unexpectedly, but sometimes you have a warning that a loved one's health is declining. You see that something is wrong, though you are not sure what. Your loved one may be in denial or resistant to go to the doctor. When you get there, the news may not be good.

Recovery is possible, but you are in for the long haul.

How much time will be spent in the hospital, surgery, rehab, ongoing physical therapy and treatment? Will there be permanent disability?

If there is loss of income, disability will only cover part of lost wages. Bills still must be paid. Life at home does not stop when someone becomes ill. Stress in the family increases as family members must spend more time with the person in need, limiting the time available to the healthy family members.

Chronic illness also comes with its own list of preparation and planning, e.g., if your or a loved one is on dialysis, travel is not impossible, but is far more difficult. In a natural disaster, people with dietary restrictions must have an emergency kit with essential supplies that can accommodate their needs. Essential medical supplies and services must be planned for. There are many guides for such planning from Medicare and/or different support groups. If you have a chronic illness or allergy, proper planning for disaster can be a matter of life or death.

Most of us have health Insurance of some kind. Some still do not have coverage. Some have lost their coverage and have struggled to replace their policy. The health insurance landscape is changing daily with the implementation of the Affordable Care Act. Your insurance policy is changing. Your co-pays and deductibles are increasing. This can create a financial crisis you were not expecting. You need help navigating the complex plans available. Where do you go for that help?

Medications can be very costly. Prescription coverage is subject to formulary approval. If your medication is not on the formulary, you may be responsible for payment in full or face a large co-pay. Entire categories of drugs may not be covered. Now what do you do?

Medical savings accounts can help you prepare for expected medical expenses not covered by your plan; e.g., braces or prescriptions not on your plan. There are many rules for these accounts. You will need help setting them up and using them properly to get maximum benefit. Your accountant can advise you of tax benefits, rules, and ramifications.

Medicare Part D has its own issues. You must find a plan that covers the drugs you take. Then, there is the "donut hole" to deal with. It can be very confusing and overwhelming for an aging parent to navigate the system to find the correct plan for them. They may need your help. Would you know what to do?

Beyond primary health insurance, do you need a gap insurance policy? If you are on Medicare, only eighty percent of your bill is covered based on a preset amount that Medicare covers. You are responsible for the remaining twenty percent. If you have a chronic illness that twenty percent can add up to big dollars you may not have.

Auto and homeowner's insurance has coverage for injuries. Though homeowner's insurance does not cover injuries to the homeowner, it does cover injury to others. Is there enough coverage to protect your family from a larger than expected judgment? Do you have an umbrella policy? Your insurance agent is a critical partner in helping you have the right coverages in place.

There are many options for disability policies as well, if you become disabled, either from an injury or illness. You can get a disability policy that will cover the difference between employer-provided disability coverage and your full salary. Some policies will even cover everything from housecleaning to dog walking while you are incapacitated. Talk to your insurance agent to make sure you have the protection you need.

So many baby boomers are now dealing with health issues, not only for themselves, but also with their aging parents. It is important to have a conversation about your parents' care well in advance of the advent of disease or disability. When Alzheimer's or dementia are factors, things can be very complicated.

Dealing with aging parents is often the alarm bell that gets the baby boomer moving toward their own complete planning for disasters involving health.

Other health-related preparation includes a healthcare proxy, a living will, and long-term care.

POINTS TO PONDER

Have you started planning for a health crisis or accident?

Have you had a conversation with your parents on the subject?

Do you know what plans your parents have in place?

Does your family know what plans you have in place?

Communication is essential.

This will insure that everyone knows what plans are in place, what your specific wishes are in the event of a medical emergency, and where to find important legal documents.

7   PREPARING FOR A HEALTH CRISIS

No one likes to think of themselves facing a health crisis.
We all want to believe we are young and healthy forever.
What can go wrong?
As it turns out, everything can go wrong. And in just a short period of time.

Every day, thousands of people find out that they have diabetes, heart disease, cancer, or an auto-immune disorder. Thousands more will have a debilitating accident. Our injured veterans returning from the battlefield have both visible and invisible injuries. Autism has increased dramatically. There are numerous mental illnesses that require continuing care. Thousands of people are waiting for organ transplants. Millions have hip, knee, and shoulder replacements every year.

Healthcare costs are spiraling ever higher as medicine and technology become more sophisticated. We are able to save tiny, premature infants and extend the quality of the lives of our elderly.

Because of the high costs associated with healthcare, we must be prepared for a health crisis.

THE BEST PREPARATION IS PREVENTION

The responsibility is on each and every one of us to do our best to take care of our bodies. Prevention is the best medicine. Your quality of life depends on it. It is never too late to use prevention.

What do I mean when I refer to prevention?

There are many things you can do to reduce your chance of becoming ill. Even if you have an existing health issue, there are things you can do to improve the quality of your health and, ultimately, your life.

Hippocrates said "Let Food Be Your Medicine"

Eating healthy foods, rich in vital nutrients is number one. A diet with an abundance of fresh fruits and vegetables and high quality protein will keep your body healthy. Protein is a key building block of muscle. Keeping your muscle-to-fat ratio at a healthy level is very important. It is more important than the number on the scale. Get a scale that can measure your percentage of body fat, percentage of muscle, percentage of visceral fat, and your BMI (body mass index).

We have an epidemic of obesity in the US. Over one-third of the population is obese. Obese children have dangerous levels of cholesterol and high blood pressure, and are showing major joint issues at younger and younger ages. We need a diet makeover —reducing sugar, fat, and carbohydrates in our diets while increasing fruits, vegetables, and protein.

The nutritional value in our foods is not what it was even twenty years ago. As a result, it is important to use quality nutritional supplements to make sure we are getting the essential vitamins, minerals, omega-3, and antioxidants our bodies need to stay healthy.

The American Medical Association understands how difficult it is to get the nutrition you need solely from the foods you eat. They recently reversed their twenty-year position on supplements. They now recommend that everyone take a multi-vitamin daily.

How do you choose the right supplements? When you go into the drug store or vitamin store, you face a wall of choices. Many advertised brands are available, but, how do you know you are absorbing the nutrients you need. Children's vitamins are a big concern. In an effort to make them palatable for children, they are laden with sugar and many use artificial flavoring and coloring that come with additional risks for developing brains and bodies.

It seems that every other month some news outlet reports that vitamins can be useless or even harmful or some doctor says do not bother taking them. Certain nutrients can be toxic or harmful if taken in high doses. Make sure you get your nutritional advice from someone who knows what they are talking about.

The truth be told, most vitamins are not worth taking. They are not absorbable and therefore any benefit from them is ending up in your toilet. Only a few companies make quality, absorbable nutritionals. One of those companies has a technology called the Bio-Photonic Scanner to measure your carotenoid levels and guarantees to increase that level with a money back offer. Carotenoids are an important measure of the health of your immune system. An article in the *Journal of the National Cancer Institute* (December 2012) published a study that concluded that women with higher carotenoid levels have a lower risk of breast cancer.

Do your own research.
Read the labels.
Ask to see third-party studies.

Beware of labels that say organic or natural as there is no standard for safety or consistency of product. Nutritional supplements are not regulated like drugs. Only you will know how much better you feel when you take them.

Finally, weight-bearing exercise three to four times a week is essential. We need to get up and move around. Our children need to get out and run and play. This keeps our metabolism revved up and our bones strong and healthy.

Prevention is your best offense in avoiding a health crisis.

NOT ALL MEDICINE IS GOOD FOR YOU

We have become accustomed to receiving prescriptions when we see doctors. Some patients even question their doctor if they do not leave with a new RX when they see them for a complaint. Medications can be highly effective but also come with risks. We have all heard the disclaimer at the end of advertisements for prescription drugs. It is important that you ask what is the drug supposed to do? Why are you taking it? How long will you need to take it? What are the potential side effects?

When you are on prescription medication, be aware of changes in your skin. Blistering, itching, and hives can be an indication of a potentially life-threatening allergic reaction. Nausea, diarrhea, and changes in digestive health should be reported to the doctor. Ace inhibitors, used in the treatment of high blood pressure and heart disease, can cause a persistent dry cough. Statins, used to lower cholesterol, can cause debilitating joint pain. Every prescription comes with a preprinted sheet with a complete listing of side effects. Oftentimes, a number of treatment choices are available, so if one drug causes discomfort, another may not. The sooner you tell your doctor about a problem, the sooner you can try something else.

When you get a prescription for a new medication do not automatically fill a ninety-day supply. Start with thirty days. If it is not the right drug for you, and you have to stop taking it, you will save money.

IMPORTANT NOTE: Sometimes doctors may prescribe several new medications at one time. If you start them at the same time and have a reaction, you will have no way to know which one caused the problem. Ask your doctor if you can start them one at a time for two to four weeks before adding the next.

Having an open discussion with your doctor is essential to get the maximum benefit from the medications you receive and help him manage your conditions the best way possible.

IMPORTANT NOTE: Disposal of Unused and Outdated Medication

Do not flush unused or outdated medication down the toilet. Medication can leach into the water supply, which can be dangerous to everyone. Likewise, medication should not be placed in the garbage. Water leaching through the landfill can find its way into the drinking water supply. Most municipalities have set up collection sites for unused and outdated medication at the police department. Find out where and how you can dispose of your medications safely.

INSURANCE FOR HEALTH AND WELLBEING

Insurance plays a major role in preparing for a health crisis.

Your health insurance policy is the foundation product in protecting your health and financial resources. Healthcare costs without health insurance is one of the leading causes of bankruptcy.

The "Affordable Care Act" sought to make health insurance accessible to everyone. So far, it has not lived up to expectations. Many who were insured have had policies cancelled and costs have risen dramatically. It has, however, removed two major problems. Pre-existing conditions no longer exclude a person from getting coverage, and there is no longer a maximum benefit ceiling. Also, young adults up to twenty-six years old are covered on their parents' policies.

You may need assistance navigating the healthcare marketplace. Reach out to people who specialize in navigating the system. Log on to Healthcare.gov to access the marketplace. Your state may have its own exchange. You can still contact insurers directly. Comparison shop to get the right plan for your needs. Be aware that there is an inverse ratio between cost and deductibles. Lower premium costs are associated with higher co-pays and deductibles, while higher premiums provide lower co-pays and deductibles. Your choice.

Research plans to make sure your doctors and medications are covered on the plan you are interested in getting.

Those on Medicare still have to make choices for their Medicare plan. Chose traditional Medicare which covers eighty percent of allowable fees charged, or choose a Medicare Advantage plan that offers enhanced benefits with possible access restrictions to network providers. Choices also must be made for Part D, prescription coverage. You can change your Part D insurer between November 1 and December 6 each year. Do not allow your prescription coverage to expire or lapse, as you will be hit with a penalty every year following the lapse in coverage.

Gap insurance policies are available that are specifically designed to cover the twenty percent that Medicare does not cover. They are reasonable and provide peace of mind that medical bills will not put undue financial stress on fixed-income seniors.

Health insurance policies still do not cover certain other health-related items. For instance, dental is not part of your health insurance coverage. You will most likely require a separate dental policy. Also not covered: braces for your children, hearing aids, eye exams, eyeglasses, or plastic surgery. You can prepare for these expenses in advance by using a medical savings account. These accounts come with their own set of tax rules and regulations. Consult your tax advisor on how best to use them.

ACCIDENT AND INJURY

Accidents happen—on the job, at home, and on the road. Where the accident occurs will determine who pays for your medical care. This can be confusing when you end up in the emergency room. The hospital wants to be paid. They will ask you where or how the injury occurred.

An accident at home for the homeowner is not covered under your homeowner's insurance. An accident at your home by someone outside the family is covered by homeowner's insurance. In either case, the injured party must present their medical insurance card at the time medical care is provided. A claim against your homeowner's policy is then initiated. Contact your insurance agent to start the process.

An accident on the job falls under compensation. The employer is required to carry state compensation insurance on their employees. Most states require that the injured party report the injury to the employer within twenty-four hours of becoming injured or compensation may be denied. You may be required to see specific doctors for evaluation of your injury and assessment of any permanent disability resulting from the on-the-job injury.

Be sure to ask contractors working at your home if they are licensed and insured. If they are not and they become injured while working on your property, you may be liable to cover their medical costs. Again, your homeowner's policy will be responsible. I also recommend you look into an umbrella policy to cover any judgment in excess of your homeowner's coverage. These policies are very reasonable and can protect the homeowner from financial ruin.

An accident on the road falls into another category. Your auto insurance covers injury and damage in an auto accident. Depending on the state, it determines whose insurance is responsible. In no-fault states, your insurance will cover you. Always get a police report. Some injuries may not be immediately apparent, e.g., whiplash injury. Notify your insurance carrier immediately. You may need to make a claim at a later date. Others involved in the accident may also make claims against your policy.

DISABILITY

If you become disabled due to illness or injury and are employed, you are covered by short-term disability insurance from your employer. Short-term disability insurance usually has a waiting period for coverage to begin and will cover you for a set maximum number of weeks. Short-term disability insurance from your employer will usually cover only half of your pay.

You can purchase additional long-term disability insurance to cover the gap between your company coverage and your regular wages. It also can extend coverage beyond the time limit of your company coverage. This can ease the financial stress of your disability on your family. Talk to your insurance agent about this additional coverage.

If your disability will permanently preclude you from returning to your job, you may qualify for Supplemental Security Income (SSI) disability benefits from the Social Security Administration. There are many specific requirements to qualify for SSI disability benefits. The Social Security Disability Benefits webpage outlines these requirements (http://www.ssa.gov/disabilityssi/ssi.html). You also can apply for your SSI disability benefits online. You will receive notices from the Social Security Administration when your application is submitted and again when your application is accepted. Once accepted, you will be interviewed by the Social Security Administration to determine if you are truly disabled and the extent of your disability. They will contact your doctors to verify the information you provided. Once approved, you will be notified of your start date and benefit amount.

Once you are on SSI disability benefits, you will be eligible for Medicare one year later. You will be notified by mail when you qualify for Medicare. Your Medicare premium will be deducted from your SSI disability payment. You will have to choose if you need Part D coverage at that time.

LONG-TERM CARE INSURANCE

If you are a baby-boomer, it is important to look at long-term care insurance. I purchased my policy when I turned fifty. Things that influenced my decision were the facts that I have no children and I have a sick husband. I wanted to know that I would have choices in my care if and when the time comes that I need it.

My parents had long-term care insurance for both of them. My father passed away at ninety, never needing it. This left my mom alone, with dementia, unable to care for herself. Having long-term care insurance has allowed her to choose a beautiful assisted living community with a secure dementia unit. This is a far better choice than being forced into a nursing home on Medicaid, requiring the forfeiture of all her assets. She is far more comfortable in her current environment. This gives both my sister and me real peace of mind, knowing that she is in a good and safe place.

There is a strong possibility that you or your spouse will someday need supervised long-term care. Long-term care insurance must be in place before you ever need it.

Most long-term care policies cover a wide variety of care options. They can include home care, assisted living, dementia care, and nursing home care. Usually, the policy provides a maximum limit per day based on level of care. There is also a maximum time limit of five years. Most seniors need care for around three years.

The price of the policy is directly related to your age at the time of purchase. There are fixed-benefit policies and policies with inflation protection built in. Pricing will vary based on the plan you choose. These policies require a health evaluation prior to their issue. Your insurance professional can help you select the right option for you.

THE LEGAL SIDE OF HEALTH CRISIS PREPARATION

For complete health crisis preparation, there are many important legal documents that should be considered. You will need to consult a legal professional to get them in place.

If you completed your legal preparation more than ten years ago, it may be time to revisit your documentation. Many states have made changes to the wording and format of the documents you need, so an update may be required. Also, laws have changed regarding trusts and living wills. Changes within your family since you prepared your documents may affect decisions you want to make for your estate. Make sure all your documents are current.

It is also important to make legal provision for care of disabled family members. This is something that needs to be addressed and discussed thoroughly to insure the safety and wellbeing of everyone in the family.

Your legal professional can guide you through the guidelines, benefits, and negatives of each option. Choose a legal professional who specializes in estate planning.

Will vs. Trust

It really depends on what your needs are. How big is the estate? What would the tax liability be to the estate? To your heirs? Do you want to protect your assets from forfeiture in case you end up in a nursing home on Medicaid?

The cost of nursing home care is more than you might expect—currently, ten to fifteen thousand dollars per month, depending on where you live. You will burn through your assets very quickly if you do not have long-term care insurance and have to pay out of pocket. That is why most people in nursing homes are on Medicaid. There is a five-year look-back for Medicaid. That is, assets need to be protected a minimum of five years before you go on Medicaid. If it has been less than five years since you took action to protect your assets–even if you passed them on to your children–the government requires that you turn those assets over to them prior to going on Medicaid.

Healthcare Proxy, Power of Attorney, and Living Wills

These are essential to have in place should you or a loved one become incapacitated. Your legal advisor can assist you with their preparation. You will be asked if you have these documents in place at every hospital admission and if you have a chronic health issue that requires treatment such as dialysis or chemotherapy.

HIPAA (Health Insurance Portability and Accountability Act)

Theoretically, this law is in place to protect your private healthcare information. It is important that you designate those people you wish to have access to your health information when you are admitted to the hospital or visit a doctor. You will be given a HIPAA form to fill out and sign. If you do not designate anyone to have access to your information, this can create unforeseen consequences.

When my mother-in-law was hospitalized in Florida, my husband called from New York to inquire on her status. Because she had not designated him for access, HIPAA laws prevented the hospital from even confirming that she had been admitted, let alone give him any status update. A parent should always designate their spouse, as well as all of their adult children, on the HIPAA form.

DNR Order

A DNR or Do Not Resuscitate Order will have to be put in place at each hospital admission. You will need your healthcare proxy and power of attorney documents to get a DNR order in place. It requires that the doctor sign off on it, as well as you or the designated power of attorney. This does not require an attorney. Note, if you approve any procedure, the DNR will be negated.

DNR means just that. If you have a DNR order in place, they will not resuscitate you if your heart or breathing stops.

It is important that you have end-of-life discussions with your loved ones. This insures that all parties know what the wishes of each loved one are. Everyone will be on the same page and allow the loved one to pass from this life the way they want to go.

Hospice Care

There may be a time that hospice care is recommended for you or your loved one. This option is recommended when the person is terminal, there is a DNR in place, and the decision has been made that the loved one is to be as comfortable as possible in their final days. Choose home hospice or hospice care in a dedicated facility. Either way, trained hospice personnel provide, twenty-four-hour care for the patient in a loving homelike environment. Feeding tubes, IVs, and other vestiges of hospital care are removed. Pain killers are administered for comfort. It is time for family members to share cherished memories and say their final goodbyes. While the patient may slip into a coma, they may still be able to hear you and know that you are there beside them. This allows the loved one to depart surrounded by those who care instead of in a hospital setting.

There are so many things to consider when addressing health, illness, and disability.

Your preparation here will help the entire family navigate the ups and downs of dealing with a wide variety of health disasters.

PLANNING PEARLS

PLANNING FOR A HEALTH CARE CRISIS

- It can happen to you, at any time.
- Prevention is the Best Medicine.
- Choose the right diet, supplements, and exercise to maintain good health.

NOT ALL MEDICINE IS GOOD FOR YOU

- Know what, why, and potential side effects of all medications you take.
- Be aware of changes that could be related to a medication.
- Discuss adding only one new prescription at a time, initially fill only a thirty-day supply.
- Properly dispose of unused and outdated medication.

ACCIDENT

- Report an on-the-job injury to your employer within twenty-four hours.
- Always get a police report and report a car accident to your insurer; many injuries do not show up immediately.

Planning Pearls (continued)

- Make sure repair people you hire are licensed and insured to avoid claims against your homeowner's policy if they become injured while working on your home.

DISABILITY

- Short-term disability usually only covers half pay.
- Find out if a long-term disability policy is right for you to protect your family.
- Investigate a gap policy such as AFLAC to cover everyday expenses.

HEALTH INSURANCE

- **Affordable Care Act.** Positive benefits: No pre-existing condition exclusion and children up to twenty-six years old can remain on parents' plan. Challenges: Rising costs, higher deductibles, and policy cancellations.
- **Medicare** pays eighty percent of allowable charges.

Planning Pearls (continued)

- **Medi-Gap** policy can cover remaining twenty percent.
- **Medicare Part D.** Prescription coverage: Shop around for best policy for your drug needs. Do not allow your Part D prescription coverage to lapse or you will have to pay penalty forever following the lapse.
- Investigate **medical savings account** for braces, Lasik eye surgery, eye care, glasses, hearing aide, and cosmetic surgery.
- **Dental Insurance** – Shop for the right policy for you.

LONG-TERM CARE INSURANCE

- Provides coverage for assisted living, dementia care, nursing home, and in-home care.
- Choose a fixed benefit or an inflation-protected policy.

Planning Pearls (continued)

LEGAL

- Choose a lawyer who specializes in estate planning Update your documents if they have been in place for more than ten years. Laws are constantly changing.
- Documents to have in place: Trust, living will, healthcare proxy, and power of attorney.
- Make legal provisions for the care of disabled family members

HIPAA

- Assign spouse and all adult children access to your healthcare information.

DNR ORDER

- New DNR order must be put in place with each hospital admission.

HOSPICE

- Choose hospice care in-home or in a dedicated facility.

8   DIVORCE

Nearly fifty percent of all marriages end in in divorce.

This is a personal disaster that can leave one or both parties angry, bitter, and completely lost. Planning in this context is not about the divorce itself, but about planning to move beyond the divorce and create a healthy environment for you and your children afterwards.

Frequently, one spouse ends up with the house. There can be constant points of contention as the little things that need to be fixed, replaced, or repaired pile up.

Who is responsible for the everyday upkeep?

What can I do if the toilet is running and when do I need to call the plumber?

What if the circuit breaker needs to be reset?

What if the drain in the bathtub is slow?

What if I want to change the lock on the door?

This parade of little things creates a never-ending string of phone calls to the absent ex-spouse. The opportunity for nagging, whining, crying, yelling, accusing, and overall bad feelings to be brought up over and over again is neither healthy nor productive in keeping a harmonious household.

What if the spouse left with the home could be more self-sufficient?
What if they were able to take care of some of the simpler tasks without engaging with the ex?
Wouldn't they be less angry, less needy, and less helpless?
Wouldn't more self-sufficiency be beneficial for all parties, especially the children?

Often a couple chooses divorce because they find living together is too disruptive for the children. But if the drama continues after the divorce, it does not help the situation.

The only way to move forward in your life is to take control of the things you can control. Feeling confident in your home is a great step to building your self-confidence. You will have a sense of being in control instead of everything spinning out of control when the smallest thing goes wrong.

Becoming self-sufficient is important to one's self esteem.

That's where a complete guide to the operation of the home is an essential tool.

Do you have such a guide in your home?

POINTS TO PONDER

FIFTY PERCENT OF MARRIAGES END IN DIVORCE.

- This is the reality we live in.

CHILDREN ARE OFTEN CAUGHT IN THE CROSSFIRE BETWEEN ANGRY PARENTS.

- There is a feeling of helplessness when little things go wrong.
- Custodial parent will lash out at non-custodial parent

THERE IS A PROFOUND LOSS OF SELF CONFIDENCE IN DIVORCE.

- Rebuild self-confidence following divorce by taking on small tasks around the house that you would have call the ex to take care of in the past.

HELPLESSESS FEEDS THE ANGER

- Empower yourself with accomplishment.
- Create a peace-filled environment for you and your children.

9 SURVIVING DIVORCE

Divorce is not easy. Beyond all the emotional ramifications, there is a labyrinth of legal hurdles to get over. Deciding who gets what, who keeps the house, custody of the children, custody of the pets, and who feels wronged and wants more retribution than the other. All this recrimination can put extreme pressure on an already tense situation.

No one is happy. A family is being ripped in half with the children in the middle. In many cases, both parents love their children so much they cannot imagine having to divide the time they spend with them. In the end, nobody wins, except maybe the lawyers who get paid before any assets are divided.

When there is such anger and hurt involved, it creates an environment that can be crippling for all parties.

The spouse who retains the house for the "stability" of the children often does not know all the ins and outs of taking care of the home.

Specifically, they may not have had any involvement with taking care of the outside, such as sprinkler maintenance, pool opening and closing, yard maintenance, snow removal, or plantings. They may not have been involved with paying the bills, taxes, and insurance premiums. They may not have first-hand experience with cleaning the bathroom, doing the laundry, cooking, or their children's schedules. They may not know what to do if a pipe leaks, the toilet overflows, the circuit breaker pops, or a tree falls on the house.

Everything changes in divorce. Without children, it is easy to walk away once the decree is signed and never talk to each other again. If there are children, you will always be connected to each other on some level.

Children are not leverage. They need to feel secure and loved more after divorce than before. They do not need to hear that their daddy or mommy did something wrong. They should never be asked to take sides or be threatened with loss of love from one parent or another. They will make up their own minds if they need to in due time.

All the little stresses of running the house can be additional points of contention between the divorced parties.

One spouse keeps calling the ex for every little thing that goes wrong:

"I don't know how."

"I can't do it."

"I need your help NOW!"

It is one emergency after another and it adds fuel to the fire.

The ex making the call may be thinking:

"How could you leave me like this?"

"You know I can't do it."

"Your children need you to do this for them."

"How can you ignore them this way?"

The ex receiving the call may be thinking:

"There he/she is again."

"Why can't they move on with their lives?"

"Why can't they figure it out?"

"I can't keep running over there for every little thing."

"Give me a break, I have a new life."

"Just do it already."

A lot of this back and forth can be eliminated. It is very empowering to be able to do something yourself. It is great for your self-confidence when you solve the problem on your own. All you need is a "How To" manual that tells you what you can do, how to do it, and when you need to call in the professionals.

Very soon, you will have access to a great resource called "The Crisis Planner," a comprehensive planning system and home operations manual. In the meantime, join our community at www.TheCrisisPlanner.com, follow our blog, and learn from others who have faced the same problems you are.

You can pick up a do-it-yourself book at any bookstore or big box hardware store. You can download instructions on how to do just about anything on the internet. Google it and more than likely you will be able to find out what you need to know.

Another option is a home warranty program. These programs provide maintenance and repair service for a wide variety of home maintenance issues. There is a manageable annual fee with moderate co-payments which can help control cost. These programs usually cover heating plant, central air, major appliances, electrical, plumbing, window and door integrity. Additional coverage can be purchased for pool and spa repairs and other specialized services. There are a number of highly rated companies to choose from. This is an option that should be explored as part of the divorce settlement.

In either case if you do-it-yourself or use a home warranty program you will build your self-confidence and self-reliance.

When your children and other family members see how well you are handling whatever life throws at you, they will be very proud of you. You will be very proud of yourself and your personal growth. You can let go of any feelings of helplessness and dependency that divorce often leaves in its wake. You will be able to move forward with your life with joy and purpose.

Life is, after all, about the journey.

PLANNING PEARLS

BUILD YOUR SELF CONFIDENCE AFTER DIVORCE.

- Start by taking baby steps around the house.
- Stop calling your ex for every little thing.
- Learn to do small things; get a do-it-yourself maintenance book.
- Ask friends for referrals for a plumber, electrician, and air conditioning/heating plant maintenance.
- Consider using a home warranty service to provide peace of mind and control cost

WHEN YOU TRY TO PUNISH THE ABSENT SPOUSE, YOU ONLY PUNISH YOURSELF AND YOUR CHILDREN.

- Your anger is not healthy for anyone, no matter how justified.

LEARN TO LET IT GO AND MOVE FORWARD WITH YOUR LIFE.

- Only then will you find happiness.
- Enjoy the journey.

10 DEATH OF A LOVED ONE

This project was born of the vision of a great man. At the age of seventy, my dad, Norbert Osiecki, watched as many of his friends and neighbors lost their spouse after many years of marriage. He observed that, in addition to the emotional devastation of the loss, there was an additional burden of dealing with the financial side and running a household by themselves.

Often, one spouse handled all the finances, while the other knew nothing. Frequently, there was a division of labor within the household. One handled the outside stuff, while the other handled the inside. Each one operated independently, yet together they worked as a well-oiled-machine. When the husband or wife died, the surviving spouse was overwhelmed with things they never had to do before.

On the home-front:

How do you close the pool?
When do the sprinklers need to be turned off?
How do you work the washing machine and the dryer?
How does the coffeepot work?

On the financial side:

How do I pay the bills?
How much money comes in each month?
Where are the insurance policies?
Who is the lawyer?
Who is the stockbroker?
Where is the safe deposit box?
What about the property taxes?
What about the income taxes?
Where is the will?
What about the computer passwords?

It was so overwhelming to deal with so many things while facing the loss itself that some sank into despair. They had no idea where to begin. This was often compounded by health issues, dementia, or Alzheimer's.

In many cases, even the adult children were not prepared to help the parent left alone. They were unable to find the important papers. They did not have essential information to help. There was a rush to make decisions. Some decisions were good and some were bad.

I am so grateful for his vision and feel his presence guiding me as I write this book and bring The Crisis Planner to life.

POINTS TO PONDER

DO YOU KNOW WHERE TO START?

AM I ASKING THE RIGHT QUESTIONS?

WHO IS ON MY TEAM?

- Lawyer
- Accountant
- Insurance Agent
- Financial Advisor

WHY IS PLANNING FOR DEATH IMPORTANT?

- This is essential to protect your family and your assets.
- There are many aspects of planning and you need to address them all.

11 SURVIVING THE DEATH OF A LOVED ONE

The death of a loved one is a traumatic life event.

It does not matter if it is sudden and unexpected or long and lingering.

Too often, people are afraid to talk about death. It is the elephant in the room. They may be superstitious and believe that if they make a plan for death, they bring it to them.

One thing that I can guarantee is that we will all die someday. No one is immune. When it is your time, death will take you, ready or not.

The grieving process is not easy. Grief includes a wide spectrum of emotions. Your feelings of sadness, fear, anger, and confusion are all normal.

The grieving process can be complicated if the surviving spouse or children are not informed and do not know where to find information. This can make a bad situation worse. It is essential to think through and plan ahead for this important final stage of life.

Do you have important legal documents in place?

Have you talked to your loved ones about your wishes?

Have you collected and recorded important information for the surviving spouse or significant other and children?

THERE ARE THREE COMPONENTS IN PLANNING FOR DEATH

The first component is planning BEFORE.

Where do you begin?

A husband and wife, or couple, should create this plan together. Communication between the parties is an essential part of planning. It is a good idea to speak with your parents to make sure they have a plan in place to protect their assets and make their wishes known.

WHO?

First, identify WHO you are planning for. Make a list of the family members and their relationship to those who are making the plan. List date of birth and date of death, if needed. These are your potential heirs. You choose who and what you wish to leave for them.

WHAT?

Second, identify WHAT. This includes the documents you need to have in place from various sources: legal, insurance, property, banking, investments, retirement income, social security, pension, funeral planning, and retirement planning. It is important to make sure to plan ahead for dependent children, disabled family members, and pets.

You need to have one place to record everything. A booklet entitled "And Now What?" allows you to record all your important information in an easy-to-read format. "And Now What?" is available on Kindle and is readable on any tablet, phone, or PC.

Order it on Amazon at:

http://www.amazon.com/dp/B00SNIGAC8

LEGAL PREPARATION

Begin with the legal preparation by recording your lawyer's name, phone, and address. List the legal documents you have in place and when they were completed and last updated. Laws change—especially trust laws—so it is important to make sure that your legal documents are in compliance with current laws. You are creating this plan to protect your assets. Make sure they are properly protected. Choose a lawyer who knows current estate planning laws. Do your own research prior to meeting with your lawyer. Write your questions down, and make a list of your assets prior to meeting with your estate planner.

Documents you will want to discuss with your estate planner are: will, trust, living will, healthcare proxy, power of attorney, and specific codicils, as necessary. You will make decisions with your estate planner that are best for your needs and that comply with the specific laws in your state.

You will get a copy of your legal documents when they are completed and signed. One signed copy will be kept on file with the lawyer. Make sure you have his contact information available for your survivors.

INSURANCE PREPARATION

Insurance is the next part of your plan. Do you have life insurance through your employer? Does your spouse? Record the name of the insured, company contact, phone, and amount for each policy. Whole or term life Insurance policies should be listed with the agent, insured's name, policy number, contact phone, provider, and the amount of the policy.

Mortgage insurance also should be listed as it often has a clause that pays the balance of the mortgage if one of the owners of the property dies. This provides protection for your spouse and your children in the event of your death.

BANKING PREPARATION

Banking information is next. Record the bank name, branch, contact phone, account number, type of account, pin numbers, safe deposit box numbers, joint ownership, and any investment accounts for each bank.

If you have a family trust, make sure that all banking, safe deposit box, and financial accounts are in the name of the family trust. Every account should have a co-signer on it. If that co-signer predeceases the owner, update the signature card to allow access to banking, investments, and safe deposit accounts.

INVESTMENT AND INCOME PLANNING

Income is the next essential part of the plan. What are your sources of income? What will they look like when one of you dies? This is important information for future planning for the surviving spouse. It is important to know where the income comes from and how much is there. Record information on Individual Retirement Accounts (IRAs), Roth IRAs, 401K accounts, Social Security, brokerage accounts, stocks, bonds, commodities, and pensions. Note where survivor benefits apply. Make sure to have all the contact information for your financial advisor and any brokerage accounts. Update beneficiary information as necessary.

FUNERAL PLANNING

Pre-planning for death: This includes information on the burial plot, mausoleum, headstone, and pre-paid funeral arrangements. In the case of your death, your family will need to know what arrangements you have made and what your requests and preferences are. It is important to note that your funeral instructions should not be in your will or trust documents as these documents are typically read weeks after death. These instructions should be left where family members will have immediate access to your wishes.

WHERE?

Where is everything?

This can be most frustrating for survivors if the deceased has not put everything together in one place. Important documents can be lost, benefits not paid, assets may lay unclaimed for years because no one knew they existed.

"ICE"

Create your **"ICE"** (in case of emergency) file on your computer desktop and in a file cabinet. Some documents must be original copies. Some require raised seals. Keys will need to be kept in the file cabinet. Many other things can be stored on the computer with your specific instructions. It is important to communicate to your loved ones how to access these files.

What goes into your "ICE" file?
IMPORTANT!

Computer Log-in and Passwords: Include information for any account that you handle online, email, Facebook, LinkedIn, Google+, Pinterest, Twitter, PayPal, banking, investment accounts, security, identity theft, AARP, AAA, credit card accounts, bill pay accounts, website, any auto-ship or auto-bill account, and cloud accounts. You can use any password keeper program you choose or one of the offline devices that allow you to keep track of your passwords. Make sure you update whatever system you choose to use whenever you make a change.

Identity Theft Protection: This is a key part of planning. Identities are frequently stolen after death. Use your discretion when posting an obituary in the newspaper. Be very careful what you post online. Identity thieves troll the newspapers and online for opportunities to steal identities. Notify credit reporting agencies of the death within a couple of days so there will be an alert for fraudulent activity under your name.

Your Last Wishes: Information on burial, mausoleum, headstone, and pre-paid funeral. Your specific requests on modest, lavish, cremation, burial, embalmed, mortuary, casket, urn, flowers, clothing, transport, service location, church, military, pallbearers, and marker.

Special Arrangements: Instructions for dependent children, disabled dependents, and pets.

Banking Information: Bank location and account numbers, safe deposit box number, location, and key.

Investment Accounts: Who, what, where, how much, contact information, account numbers. Stock and bond certificates. Gold, silver, platinum bullion type and location.

Legal Documents: Lawyer's name and contact number, copies of documents in place.

Insurance Policies: Copies of all life insurance, long-term care insurance, homeowner's insurance, mortgage insurance, and umbrella insurance policies should be collected. Health insurance policies, Medicare information, secondary health insurance, or catastrophic policies for accident, and disability are part of your insurance information. Finally, do not forget your auto insurance, as well as specialty policies for boats, RVs, motorcycles, ATVs, trailers, or any other items. Include contact names and numbers for each of your insurance agents.

Real Property Documents: Mortgage, deed, title, survey, and COs (certificate of occupancy) for each property. Include any timeshare or vacation share properties.

Titles: Auto, boat, motorcycle, RV, trailer, or ATV, as required by your state.

Other Important Documents: Birth certificates, marriage license, divorce degree, death certificates, passports and passport numbers, driver's license copies and numbers, copy of pistol permits with list of licensed handguns.

List of High Value Collectables: Including who you want to have each item.

Cash: Stash location.

Once you have assembled everything in your ICE file it is essential to keep things up to date. Whenever anything changes, place the new document in the file and remove anything that no longer applies.

Now you are ready to face whatever comes your way. Your family and assets are protected.

The second component of planning for death occurs UPON the death itself.

This is an important emotional and vulnerable time for the surviving partner, spouse, or children. They will have to make many decisions. Some decisions will have to be made quickly. Thankfully, many decisions can wait.

Immediately Upon Death

- Get a pronouncement of death. If death occurs in the hospital or under hospice care, the doctor or hospice worker can pronounce. If the death occurs at home, not under hospice care, you must call 911. If you do not have a DNR (Do Not Resuscitate) order in hand when they arrive, they will be required to attempt resuscitation. They will question those in the household regarding the circumstances of the death. Only when paramedics or medical examiner pronounce will CPR cease and the body be removed. This can be a frightening and intimidating experience.

- Once the body is released and if no autopsy is required, call the funeral home to have the body transported. Notify the doctor or the coroner. Notify close family and friends. Arrange care of dependents and pets. Call the employer and request information on death benefits.

- Open the **ICE** (in case of emergency) file on the computer and locate the file in the file cabinet. Read written instructions for the funeral and burial or cremation.

- Call the three credit agencies and put a fraud alert on the social security number to prevent identity theft.

Within a Couple of Days of Death

- Make an appointment to meet with the funeral director. Bring a family member or trusted friend with you. Arrange for funeral and burial or cremation. Confirm all pre-paid arrangements with the funeral home.

- If no advance arrangements have been made, there are many things to discuss and plan. Use any instructions and specific requests from the deceased.

- First, discuss your budget. Next, the burial or cremation, casket or urn, viewing room, dates and times, open or closed casket. If applicable, arrange a military tribute at the funeral home or gravesite. Identify special remembrances, the verse for the remembrance card, clothing for viewing and burial, flower arrangements from the family, transportation, religious service, donation amount, time, date, location, readings, music, eulogy (yes/no and who will read it and where). Request twenty-five to thirty copies of the death certificate. Get an itemized bill and plan the post-burial meal.

- If the deceased was a member of the military, police department, fire department, a union, a fraternal organization, or a religious group, contact that organization. They may have death benefits.

- Arrange to have a trusted friend or relative watch the house, answer the phone, collect the mail, and water plants.

- Run a final credit report from all three credit agencies.

- Keep the primary credit card open.

- Punch a hole in the driver's license and passport.

- Collect paperwork for insurance policies.

5 MISTAKES TO AVOID

1. Do not turn off the phone.
2. Do not cancel the primary credit card.
3. Do not notify everyone immediately.
4. Avoid posting an obituary in the newspaper or on Facebook. Robbers and identity thieves troll the obituary pages and internet for new targets.
5. Do not make any major life decisions right away. You need time to absorb the changes in your life. Things will look different a week or a month from now.

Within 10 Days of the Death

- Obtain death certificates from the funeral home. Start with twenty-five to thirty copies. You will need a copy for each financial institution, insurance policy, government agency, investment, and brokerage account.

- Contact the lawyer for the reading of the will and filing with the appropriate county, state, or city office for probate, if necessary. Learn how to transfer assets to the survivor. The executor should open a bank account for the deceased's estate, as necessary.

- Contact the police, if the house is empty, for a periodic drive-by.

- Contact the accountant to find out when a tax return needs to be filed.

- Contact the bank to update signature cards for bank accounts and safe deposit box.

- Contact the insurance agent for life insurance claim forms.

- Contact the Social Security Administration at 800-772-1213 or online at socialsecurity.gov.

- Contact Veterans Affairs at 800-827-1000 or online at VA.gov

- STOP PAYMENTS, FILE FOR DEATH BENEFITS, AND FIND OUT ABOUT SURVIVOR BENEFITS.

IMPORTANT NOTE: If you have received a Social Security payment for the month of the death, that money will have to be returned.

- Contact the pension service; notify them of the death.

- Change the name on all utilities accounts as necessary.

The final component of planning for death is AFTER.

"After" is all about the healing. You need to take the time to grieve. Your friends and family will be close immediately following the loss. After the burial, you may feel abandoned as others return to their daily routine. You may not feel up to doing anything or you may want to dive back in to anything that feels normal. There is no right or wrong way to grieve.

Cry, laugh, feel angry, lonely, sad, confused, overwhelmed, frustrated, afraid, or freed. Your feelings are real and it is okay to express them.

Do not, however, lock yourself away from family and friends. Reach out and talk. Talk about the positive. Share the happy memories and the progress you made that day. You will have good days and bad days. You will move forward three steps then two steps back. This is all normal.

Day by day, things should start to improve. You should be able to go back to work. If you do not work, you can return to your normal routine.

If you start to feel depressed and you cannot seem to shake it, you may benefit from bereavement counseling in an individual or group setting. Bereavement groups can be found through your church, funeral director, visiting nurse service, or hospital. Individual counseling can be found through psychotherapy services.

Life will be different after a loss. This is for sure. But be assured that your life is not over.

Who you are is not defined by whose child you were or who you were married to.

You have special unique gifts to discover and share with the world.

So, when you ask yourself "And Now What?" you might just be surprised at the answer.

PLANNING PEARLS

THERE ARE THREE PARTS OF YOUR PLAN FOR DEATH: *Before, Upon, and After.*

KEY AREAS FOR PLANNING: *Legal, Insurance, Financial, and Funeral*

- Create your ICE file. Keep all your information together.

- Advise your family where they can find and how to access important information.

- Keep a list of log-in and passwords for every online account; include that list in your ICE file.

- Protect your identity following death. Family must notify credit reporting agencies, Social Security, VA, and file income taxes per your accountant.

- Keep last wishes in your ICE file for immediate access.

Planning Pearls (continued)

AVOID 5 MISTAKES

1. Do not turn off the phone.
2. Do not close all credit cards.
3. Do not call everyone immediately.
4. Avoid posting an obituary and in social media if possible.
5. Do not make major life decisions right away.

THERE IS LIFE AFTER A LOSS.
SEEK SUPPORT IF YOU NEED TO.

12 THERE ARE SOME THINGS THAT YOU CANNOT PLAN FOR

There are some personal disasters in life for which there can be no planning.

These are the things that happen that we do not want to think about.

They are considered to be too awful to contemplate. Yet, too many people experience these things to ignore them. They bring with them significant pain. Recovery can seem difficult and, for some, even impossible.

I would be remiss if I did not address these personal disasters and the impact on those affected by them. This discussion is designed to bring awareness that family and friends may be hurting deeply. I also hope that I can provide an opportunity for you to open communication and provide love and support during a time of great loss.

MISCARRIAGE

This is very common, and the loss the woman feels is profound. There are so many feelings that wash over you. You feel sad, depressed, guilty, and angry. If you had not yet announced your pregnancy, others may not be aware of your loss at all. If you had announced it to family and friends, they do not know what to say, or how to support you. When they say they are sorry, they mean it. When they say you can try again, you somehow feel betrayed. Betrayed by them, by your body, and by God. Some will not know what to say. So they say nothing, which feels like no one cares.

The sadness is compounded by the wave of hormones changing back to a non-pregnant state. You cry. You cannot stop crying. For most women, these feelings slowly recede. You will be able to move on with your life.

Many women have experienced multiple miscarriages, but it is never expected. With each miscarriage, the feelings of loss compound.

The sadness and feelings of inadequacy can be so profound, it is easy to fall into a depressive state. Many support groups and individual counseling are available to help you navigate through the darkness into the light once again.

STILLBIRTH

You have carried a baby for nine months and, prior to your due date, your baby dies while still in the womb. You have to endure labor and delivery, but there is no infant crying, no baby placed in your arms. Because it was not a live birth, there is no funeral, no closure. You may have prepared a nursery in your home. There may have been a baby shower. Once you come home, there are reminders everywhere that you lost something—someone—very real.

Your heart is broken. Your arms ache with the emptiness you feel. Your husband and family try to say the right things. But for you, nothing feels like it will ever be right again. You feel like everyone is looking at you and pitying you. Just as with miscarriage, many people do not know what to say. They can say stupid things that hurt without the intention to do so. Your feelings are genuine. Allow yourself to go through the grieving process. Cry your eyes out and be angry. Do not be afraid to reach out to support groups or counseling services available in the community.

DEATH OF AN INFANT OR CHILD

No matter when the death occurs, all is not right with the world. If your child dies soon after birth or at any time afterwards, it is not in the natural order of things. Your child is supposed to outlive you; you are not supposed to have to bury your child. This is true even if your child is long grown and an adult in their fifties.

Most people typically know what to do when a funeral occurs. That being said, it is particularly difficult in the case of an infant or young child. There are those who may not be able to deal with it. They may opt not to come because it is too difficult for them. They are not trying to slight you.

Others may say the wrong things, without malicious intent. Words meant to comfort can be so hurtful. Seek support if you need it. Bereavement support is available in many locations through church, your local visiting nurse service, hospice, and individual counseling.

SUICIDE

When a spouse, child, family member, or friend commits suicide, we are always surprised initially. Then we start to think about the "messages" the person had been sending us and the world. We feel guilty for not picking up on the sadness or for not being there when they needed us.

We are dealing with a loss of a loved one but, at the same time, we blame ourselves for somehow allowing it to happen.

It is not your fault.

There is nothing you could have done to change the outcome.

Moving forward with your own life following a loved one's suicide carries with it the same wide range of emotions that are felt with every loss and death. If you are having a difficult time, reach out to friends, family, group and individual counseling as needed.

MURDER

When a family member is murdered, the loss is always sudden and unexpected.

Murder can occur as the result of a crime, an act of terrorism, or an act of war.

Adding to the emotional roller coaster is the police and legal intervention to identify, charge, and prosecute the perpetrator. During the initial investigation, family members may be interrogated. Homes, cars, and places of business may be searched. Your life may be turned upside down and inside out during this process. You will not be able to bury your loved one or plan a funeral until the autopsy is completed.

Your entire life will be in limbo. You will not be able to start the grieving process until you know the who and why of the murder itself. For some, there are no answers. The case remains unsolved. There is no closure. It remains an open wound for years and years.

If they charge someone with the crime, there will be a trial. During the trial, you will relive every gruesome detail of how your loved one was taken from you. They may drag your loved one's life and reputation through the mud to create a defense. This is not fair to the victim and the victim's family. It is, however, the American system of justice. You are innocent until proven guilty. If the accused is found guilty, the sentence may seem inadequate compared to the loss you feel. If they are found not guilty, you will feel that there is no justice.

There are specific groups to support families of murder victims. Join one to help you with the anger and helplessness you feel.

In the case of both suicide and murder, there is little we can do to prepare for the emotional impact these events will have.

As an adult, you should have some plans in place. The same legal, financial, insurance, and funeral planning you have done for the event of natural death and for natural disasters should be in place to protect your family even in the event of a suicide or murder.

It is important to know that you are not alone. Many others have faced the same nightmare. They have sought help when they needed it. Some have turned their nightmare into providing support for others who have faced the same thing.

You can recover.
Your life will go on.
The quality of your life afterwards is up to you.

You can wither and withdraw from life or you can find joy once again and thrive.

POINTS TO PONDER

PREPARING FOR THE UNTHINKABLE:

- Miscarriage
- Stillbirth
- Death of an Infant or Child
- Suicide
- Murder

Seek counseling and join support groups to help you deal with the emotional aftermath.
Give yourself permission to grieve.
Forgive those who may not know what to say or who say the wrong thing unintentionally

ADULTS SHOULD HAVE PLANS IN PLACE:

- Legal
- Insurance
- Financial
- Funeral

THERE IS LIFE AFTER THESE EVENTS OCCUR.
THE CHOICE IS YOURS AS TO HOW YOU RECOVER.

13 GUIDING AGING PARENTS THROUGH THE PLANNING PROCESS

Now that I have your attention and you are motivated to move forward with your planning process, I have to ask you . . .

. . . Are your parents prepared?

Do they have their final plans in place?

Have they communicated those plans to you and your siblings?

If one parent should die, could you help the remaining parent through the changes they now face?

Would you know where to find important papers?

Would you know what their final wishes are?

Do you know if they have protected their assets?

Do they have a long-term care insurance policy for the remaining parent, if necessary?

So many questions.

How do you bring the discussion up if you have never had it before?

This can be a delicate conversation to broach. If your parents have not spoken of their final plans before, there can be many reasons. They may be afraid that you are after their "money." They may be

117

afraid that you will put them in a home. They may have trust issues with one or more of their children. They may feel that talking about end-of-life planning will bring bad things to them.

You must bring up the conversation in a non-threatening way. You may start the conversation by sharing what you are doing to set up your own plan. Do not overwhelm them with the whole story. Share that you have spoken to an estate lawyer to set up your own trust documents. Lead them into the conversation by saying, "I never realized how important these legal documents are." Share the benefit of creating a trust, i.e., to protect assets for the surviving spouse in the event that one of them becomes infirm and requires nursing home care. Maybe share that a nursing home can cost ten to fifteen thousand dollars a month. That is why people in nursing homes are frequently on Medicaid. Remind them that there is a five-year look-back on assets. Tell them how grateful you are that you are creating your trust now.

Now that you have set the stage, ask them if they have a will or trust in place? Let the conversation go where it will. If they have a trust in place, you will know. If they do not, ask them if they would like to talk to the lawyer who is helping you. Offer to make the introduction for them.

Slowly, you can introduce other aspects of planning such as insurance, financial, income, investment, banking, final wishes, and creating an ICE file.

If they are already facing a health crisis or if one parent has passed, there is greater urgency. There may be situations of dementia or Alzheimer's. It is essential to get a power of attorney and a healthcare proxy in place before the condition progresses to a point that they can no longer legally consent and sign these documents. Waiting too long could make it necessary to get them declared incompetent before those documents can be put in place.

If you simply do not know how to approach your parents or what to say, consider showing them a copy of the booklet "And Now What?," a planning guide and survivor's checklist for what to do before, upon, and after the death of a loved one. Give your parents a copy of this simple-to-use, fill-in-the-blank book, or mail it to them with a note. Tell them, "I just found this great little planning booklet. I'm using it for my plan and thought it would be something you would like."

Order your copy of "And Now What?" at www.TheCrisisPlanner.com or get your Kindle version on Amazon: http://www.amazon.com/dp/Boo5NIGAC8.

The booklet will take them step-by-step through all the parts of their plan. It will help them set up an ICE file to keep everything together. It also will walk them through what to do when their spouse passes.

Remember when you bring up this conversation to speak from the heart.

Speak out of love.

Do not scold them if they have not planned yet.

Offer to help, if they need it.

Congratulate them if they have completed everything already and help them collect the information in an ICE file. Use "And Now What?" as a checklist.

Talk about planning for their funeral. What do they want? What don't they want?

This is about communication.

This is about family.

This is about your love for them and wanting to protect them through proper preparation.

This is the most important conversation you can have with your parents.

PLANNING PEARLS

Gently bring up the topic of planning with your parents.

Do they have plans in place?

Are their plans complete?

Give them a copy of **"And Now What?"** to guide them through the planning process. Have a conversation about their final wishes; have them put their wishes in writing. Help them collect their documents in an "ICE" file.

Key legal documents include:

- Trust – In place minimum of five years to protect assets.
- Power of Attorney and Healthcare Proxy – Especially important in the event of dementia or Alzheimer's; have in place before parent is incompetent to make legal decisions.
- Long-Term Care Insurance

Speak from a place of caring, love, and protecting them in the event of a health crisis or death.

14 MILITARY DEPLOYMENT

I am so grateful to the brave men and women in the military for their service. They give up so much so that I can be safe and free. My simple words of thanks seem so inadequate compared to their sacrifice.

Since 9/11 members of the military have been asked to do so much. Many have been deployed numerous times to Iraq and/or Afghanistan. Each deployment takes them away from their families and puts their lives in danger.

Each deployment comes with the risk of being killed in the line of duty.

Each deployment carries a risk of being injured and/or permanently disabled.

Each deployment increases the risk of post-traumatic stress disorder (PTSD).

Each deployment makes it harder to reintegrate into life upon their return.

These brave, committed men and women go willingly into the danger zone. They get so little for the risks they take. They endure low pay, horrific living conditions in the field, and see things that will live in their nightmares for a lifetime.

Yet, there is nothing else that they would rather do.

Their families deserve as much credit. They stay home and support their loved one's decision to serve. They fear the worst every day. Yet, they pray for and believe that their loved one will come home unharmed.

There are additional considerations when a single-parent is deployed. So much preparation is necessary to insure that the children are safe and well cared for during a deployment lasting many months. The deployed parent wrestles with the fear and guilt of leaving their children behind.

The military has many planning tools to ensure that things run smoothly at home during deployment.

Is it enough?

What else is needed?

What else can family, friends, and community do to support our deployed service members?

POINTS TO PONDER

Military deployment has many risks:

- Death
- Injury/Disability
- PTSD
- Difficulty in Reintegration

Single-parent families have special needs for pre-deployment preparation.

The military helps in preparation for deployment.

Is it enough?

What else is needed?

How can family, friends, and community help?

15 PREPARING FOR MILITARY DEPLOYMENT

Military deployment causes a major disruption in family life.

Deployment is a reality for members of our military. Active duty, Reserve, and National Guard can all be called for deployment at any time. Sometimes the notice allows enough time to prepare. Other times, they are called up on short notice with very little time for them and their families to prepare.

If you are a member of the military you should be ready for the possibility that you can be called to deploy at any time. You and your family should have a comprehensive plan in advance of that event.

The military has put in place many excellent support tools to help their members prepare for deployment.

These tools are very important for you and your family's wellbeing.
Do not circular file them.
Do not tuck them away in a drawer.
Read them, understand them, and use them to create your personal plan for your family in the event of deployment.

WHAT ARE THE COMPONENTS OF PLANNING FOR DEPLOYMENT?

Financial Planning

Have a clear understanding of your income and expenses

Plan for and protect your savings; you should aim for saving fifteen percent of your income.

Make sure your family has access to all of your accounts.

- Online banking access
- Joint accounts
- Cosigners on accounts – choose spouse, parent, caregivers of dependent children, or close relatives

Get additional help to manage finances if necessary at:

- Military One Source
- Personal Financial Management Programs
- MyMoney.gov

Protect Your Property

Update your insurance policy.

Notify insurance company if your home will be unoccupied.

Get insurance coverage for personal property if you need to put belongings in storage.

Get renter's insurance.

Contact your auto insurance agent to see if your premium can be reduced.

Secure storage of your vehicle, if necessary.

Life Insurance

Service-members Group Life Insurance (SGLI) – Get a maximum coverage policy.

National Guard and Reserve may qualify for additional coverage based on income.

Legal Preparation

Your legal preparation should include a will or trust document, power of attorney, living will, arrangements for dependent children, guardianship, executor, and last wishes. Advise family where these documents are in the event something happens to you.

ICE (In Case of Emergency) File

Create a file where you keep all your important papers together for your family to access if necessary. Include your financial, investment, insurance, legal, mortgage papers, rental agreements, car loans, title documents, copy of passport, driver's license, computer passwords, banking information, and final wishes. Tell your spouse or your trusted family member or friend where to find the file if needed.

Planning to Keep Your Children Safe

This is probably the most important and the most challenging part of the planning process. This is difficult enough when you are leaving your children behind with your spouse and can be even more complex for a single parent. It is essential that you know that your children will be financially secure while you are gone. Sometimes they will need to relocate during your deployment to insure that they are in a safe environment. These are important decisions that must be discussed with your spouse and other family members who may have to assist in your absence.

Single parents and those responsible for a disabled spouse, parent, or other family member must have a family care plan in place. The same is true when both parents are in the military in either active, reserve, or National Guard status. Your family care plan is your backup plan for the "What Ifs" of life and death.

Every military member should have an informal family care plan, at the very least. This plan should be discussed thoroughly and shared with your deployment home-front battle buddy. This is the person who will be able to speak for you and your wishes in the event that you are unable to communicate while deployed.

Single parents are faced with additional challenges.

They must choose a caregiver for their children. This should not be taken lightly by either party. You cannot assume that the person you would most like to be your children's caregiver will be willing or able to take on the task. You have to ask yourself and the potential caregiver important questions.

What is the state of their health?

Depending on the caregiver's age, will they be able to keep up with the demands of an infant or toddler. Will they be able to cope with the moody teenager or support the crazy activity schedule your children may have with sports and activities?

Is you caregiver still working, and how will that interfere with or support their new role?

Will the caregiver be able to relocate to your home for the duration of your deployment or will your children have to relocate to their home, change schools, leave friends, and activities?

What are your choices for selecting a caregiver for your children while deployed?

Grandparents – Willing, age, health, activity level, working, financial situation, location?

Have a heart-to-heart conversation. While deployment is temporary, there are risks and potential consequences. Again ask the "what ifs." What if you are injured, disabled, or killed during deployment? What then? What support can they give in the event of PTSD?

Sibling, Friend, or Other Trusted Family Member – Ask the same questions as above. Have a real conversation about all the possible outcomes of deployment.

Non-Custodial Parent – Consult with an attorney to safeguard your custody while deployed. While not ideal, for some, this may be the only option.

There is a great need for childcare assistance for deployed military. There is help through child, youth, and school services for Army, Navy, Marines, National Guard, and Coast Guard.

For those caring for special needs family members, there is limited availability of free hourly childcare and respite care programs. These are available for families of deployed soldiers.

Reaching out is a sign of courage and strength.

There are many support resources available prior to military deployment. Tap into these resources for everything with which they can assist you.

- "Plan for Your Deployment" at http://www.military.com/military-report/plan-for-your-deployment

- www.militaryonesource.mil/deployment

- USAA.com

- "Plan for Financial Readiness Before Deployment" at www.realwarriors.net/guardreserve/treatment/finances.php

- Military OneSource Tips at http://www.militaryonesource.mil/tips

- Operation Military Kids at http://www.operationmilitarykids.org/public/home.aspx

- Deployment Health and Family Readiness Library at http://deploymenthealthlibrary.fhp.osd.mil/

- "Coming Home: A Guide for Spouses of Service Members Returning from Mobilization/deployment" at http://support.militaryfamily.org/site/DocServer?docID=161

- Pre-Deployment Checklist for Family Members at http://www.jag.navy.mil/legal_services/docu ments/Pre-deployment%20Checklist.pdf

- Active Duty Single Parents Deployment Readiness Checklist at http://www.vp4.navy.mil/deployment/Single_ Parent_Deploy_Checklist_Final.pdf

Other resources are available within your community and through your church. Use every resource you can. This is about your family and they deserve all the help they need while you are gone. I repeat: Reaching out is a sign of courage and strength.

As a member of the military, you owe it to yourself and your family to create a complete plan for any disaster you can face. Creating your plan will give you peace of mind. You will know your family is safe and will be taken care of, no matter what happens. You will be able to focus on the tasks of your deployment without distractions, so that you can return home safely.

I thank you for your service and sacrifice.

PLANNING PEARLS

Preparing for military deployment is essential to protect your family.

Aspects of planning include:
- Financial
- Securing your Property
- Insurance
- Legal
- ICE (In Case of Emergency) File
- Creating your Family Care Plan
- Having a Home-front Battle Buddy

Choose your caregiver carefully. Are they ready, willing, and able to take on the responsibility, short or long term? If you must use a non custodial parent as a caregiver while deployed consult an attorney to safeguard your custody while deployed

Use all the resources available to you from the military, community, and church.

16 DON'T SWEAT THE SMALL STUFF

It is important to remember, it is all small stuff.

There are so many little things that can cause chaos in your life.

There are a million things that can go wrong on any given day.

The toilet can overflow.
A pipe could leak.
You may need to hang curtains.
You may have to replace a light bulb.
Your car can break down.
You could lose your house key.
A window can break.
The power could go out.
Your chimney could be blocked.

Shit happens. . . .

It never happens at a good time. You are always rushing out the door or you have to be somewhere else when the basement fills with water. Company is on the way when the oven quits. You are all alone when the power goes out.

Do you know what you can do yourself?
Do you know how you can minimize the damage?

Do you know when to call in the professional?
Do you know who to call for help?

Your first instinct may be to call your spouse or parents for help. But Mommy and Daddy may not always be available when you need help. You may not live close to your parents, making it impossible for them to help even if they wanted to. Your spouse may be at work, so you may need to deal with the issue yourself. No need to panic. Like I said, it's all small stuff.

Three Important Things You Need to Know

1. If it involves water leaking – Label and know where the water shut off is. If you cannot isolate the source, turn off the main valve. This will stop the flow of water. Then you can call the plumber.

2. If it involves gas - i.e., you smell gas in the house, leave the house immediately. Call the fire department and the gas company once you are outside. If flooding is near the gas hot water heater or your gas heating plant, there is a risk that your pilot light will go underwater. Label and know where the gas shut off is, usually outside. Turn off the gas to prevent possibility of fire when the water issue is resolved. You may have to call the gas company to restart your appliances.

3. If it involves electrical – Know where your circuit breakers are located. Make sure you have them labeled so that you can reset them or turn them off as necessary. Again, if flooding is involved and there is a risk of shock to you, do not attempt to work with the electrical panel.

Most everything else can wait for you to fix it yourself or until a professional gets there.

There are many do-it-yourself books that can help you address all these little problems.

A good home operation guide can walk you through what you can do and when to call for the professionals. You can develop your own list of trusted professionals to call when you need to. You will need to keep that list handy so that you are not scrambling to find someone when a disaster occurs. There are a number of home warranty companies that provide maintenance and service for your home as part of an annual contract with relatively small service call costs. This can provide you with peace of mind and cost control.

Just take a deep breath, everything will be okay.

POINTS TO PONDER

There are a million little things that can go wrong.
It is all small stuff.

THREE EXCEPTIONS:

- Water leaking – Stop the flow of water then call the plumber.

- Gas – Leave the house immediately. Call the fire department and gas company.

- Electrical – Pull the main breaker (if no water is nearby). Call an electrician.

A DO-IT-YOURSELF MANUAL OR HOME WARRANTY CAN BE YOUR BEST FRIEND.

17 TAKING CARE OF THE SMALL STUFF

How can you prepare yourself for the thousands of things that could go wrong around the house?

How do you know what and when to do specific activities to prevent problems?

How can you control the cost of routine and emergency maintenance?

There are a lot of things you can do to help yourself. Preparing for the little disasters of home ownership involves awareness.

Identify your water shut-off and gas shut-off valves. Label them for use in an emergency.

Find your electrical panel. Label your main breaker and circuit breakers so you know which beaker turns what circuit on and off.

THE WALK-AROUND

Now walk around your house going room to room.

Where are the fire/smoke detectors?

Change your batteries in your fire detectors two times a year. If you do it when the time changes, you will never forget. If your fire/smoke detector is hard-wired as part of your security system find out how you can test that the monitoring and notification portion is working. Call your security company to conduct a test.

Where is your carbon dioxide (CO_2) detector/s? Check when it expires and record it in your ICE file. Replace your CO_2 detector, as necessary. Maintenance of these seemingly small devices can save your life.

Check out your bathrooms. Is there a ground fault interrupter (GFI) outlet? A GFI is an outlet with a built-in, push-button, reset switch designed to protect you from electrical shock. When there is no power in the bathroom, the GFI outlet may be in the off position. GFIs are typically found in bathrooms, kitchens, and outside outlets. These locations have a high risk of being compromised with water, creating a high risk of electrical shock. If there is no water near the outlet, simply reset the switch and the power should come back on. If your bathroom outlet is not a GFI, you may want to have it upgraded by an electrician.

While in the bathroom, identify the water shut-off for the toilet and the sink. Keep a plunger next to the toilet so that, in case of a clog, you can clear it quickly. If the toilet is overflowing or constantly running, you can turn off the water and minimize the damage. Water leaks in bathroom plumbing can create significant damage if not detected and stopped immediately. That constantly running toilet can cause your septic system to fill and back up into your house in a matter of hours. Being able to turn the water off is very important no matter the cause.

Check the caulking around the tub and shower enclosure. If it is cracked, flaking, or missing you have a high risk of water getting behind your tile or shower enclosure and ruining the wallboard behind it. Water can run down the wall and along the floor beams. In a two-story home, it can soak through the ceiling below, causing the ceiling to collapse. You can re-caulk your tub easily and avoid any potential damage.

Next, check out the kitchen. Is there a GFI outlet next to the sink? If not, consider having one installed. You should have a GFI outlet in the kitchen for the same reasons you should have one in the bathroom.

How many outlets do you have in the kitchen? Are they all on the same circuit? Many countertop appliances use a lot of amps. It is easy to overload a circuit if you have a coffeemaker, toaster, and waffle iron all in use at the same time. This can cause your circuit breaker to blow. Reduce the load on the circuit and reset the breaker. You can have additional circuits installed by a licensed electrician.

Find the water shut-off under the sink. Your dishwasher, water filter, and refrigerator line may all feed off the water line to the sink. Any one of these can be a source for a leak. It is easy to turn off the water under the sink and stop the leak quickly.

Kitchen fires are a primary source of house fires. There are risks of fire from gas, the oven, grease, and compromised wiring. You should keep a fire extinguisher, specifically for kitchen fires, under the kitchen sink. Fire extinguishers have inspection and expiration dates on them. Make sure to check those dates and replace or recharge as necessary. These are single-use extinguishers. If you use it, even briefly, you need to replace it or recharge it. Inspect the wiring of any countertop appliance before you use it. Countertop appliances should be unplugged for safety when not in use.

Walk through the rest of the house. Make sure cords are not running under carpeting. Make sure that outlets are not overloaded. Install surge protectors for your electronics, computers, and televisions to protect them from fluctuations in current.

If you have a fireplace or wood stove, protect your flooring or carpeting in front of the hearth with a flame-resistant covering. Keep flammable products away from the area. Get your chimney cleaned at least once a year. Depending on the amount of use, it may need to be cleaned twice. This will prevent chimney fires.

Identify any broken or cracked windows. You should have them repaired to keep your heating or cooling inside. Drafty windows and doors may need to have weather-stripping applied. Most hardware stores sell easy-to-use kits to do this yourself.

Finally, walk around the outside of the house.

Where are your outside faucets? Is there a danger of freezing in the winter? You will need to find and label the shut-off inside the house for these faucets. Once turned off, open the outside valve to keep them from freezing. Your sprinkler system may need to have regular maintenance. If you have cold winters, the system needs to be turned off and the lines blown out to prevent freezing in the fall. In springtime, the system will need to be turned on and checked for leaks. You should have a professional sprinkler maintenance person do this for you.

Seasonal swimming pools will need to be closed and opened each year. You can do this yourself, although it is a lot of work. A reliable pool company can close the pool, blow out the lines, and open it again for summer.

Check out the gutters. Are they clear? Gutters that are clogged with leaves and other debris can result in damage to your roof and the interior of your home. Clean them yourself or hire someone to clean them for you.

Evaluate the condition of your driveways and walkways. How does the roof look? Are the chimney flashings lying flat on the roof?

Your walk-around will show you that there are lots of things you can control and take care of yourself. It will not be nearly as scary when something does goes wrong. You will feel confident and competent to deal with an emergency when you are faced with one.

Many hardware stores offer clinics on things you can do yourself. There are many do-it-yourself books that can guide you through minor projects. It is up to you how much you want to take on and how much you want to learn.

If you don't have an electrician, plumber, sprinkler maintenance, pool maintenance, air conditioning repairman, or heating plant person that you are comfortable with, ask your friends or family members for referrals or use a reliable referral company such as Angie's List or Home Advisor to find reliable, licensed, and insured people to work on your home.

Look into a home warranty service. Home warranty typically covers heating, central air, major appliances, electrical, plumbing, and door and window integrity. Having a home warranty in place can provide peace of mind and control repair costs.

Very soon a new resource will be available called The Crisis Planner. It includes a comprehensive home operations manual as well as essential planning tools. Join our community at www.TheCrisisPlanner.com to receive the latest updates on availability.

Knowledge is power. With even a small amount of knowledge, you can feel more comfortable when dealing with the little things that can go wrong around your home

Remember, don't sweat the small stuff. In the end, it is all small stuff.

PLANNING PEARLS

IDENTIFY AND LABEL:

- Gas shut-off
- Water shut-off
- Circuit breakers

MAINTAIN YOUR FIRE/SMOKE DETECTOR:

- Change batteries two times a year.

Inspect and replace CO_2 detectors as required.
A home walk around will keep you aware of small things before they become big problems

BATHROOM

- Check for GFI outlet (If you don't have one, get one for safety).
- Check for leaks under the sink and behind toilets.
- Re-caulk sinks and tub/shower, as necessary, to prevent water damage.

Planning Pearls (continued)

KITCHEN

- Check for GFI outlets near sink (If you don't have one, get one for safety).
- Check for leaks under the sink.
- Keep a fire extinguisher, specifically for kitchen use, under the sink.

REST OF HOUSE

- Check for overloaded circuits, fireplace/wood stove safety, window and door integrity.

OUTSIDE THE HOME

- Inspect roof, flashings, and gutter integrity.
- Protect the sprinkler system, outdoor faucets, and seasonal pools from freezing.
- Inspect walkways and outdoor lighting for safety.

HAVE A GOOD DO-IT-YOURSELF MANUAL.

Planning Pearls (continued)

GET REFERRALS:

- For a competent plumber, electrician, or someone to do AC/heating plant, sprinkler, and pool maintenance, use a reliable referral or home warranty service.

GET CONNECTED WITH THE CRISIS PLANNER COMMUNITY

- www.TheCrisisPlanner.com.

DON'T SWEAT THE SMALL STUFF. . . .

18 WHAT ARE YOU WAITING FOR?

You know you need to plan for disasters in life. You know the benefit of having plans in place to protect you and your loved ones. You know that "Shit Happens." Yet, you would allow yourself to be caught with no plan in place.

Why does this happen? Do you think you put yourself in danger by having a plan? Do you believe that you can wing it? Do you think that it will never happen to you? Do you believe it is no big deal? Or does it seem so overwhelming that you just keep putting it off?

STOP!

Disaster can strike without warning at any time. Accidents happen. Health issues and death occur every day. The consequences of not having a plan can be devastating.

It's time to get your disaster plan in place.

If planning seems overwhelming, all you need to do is follow a step-by-step guide to get all the pieces of an effective plan in place.

151

One piece at a time.

Check it off the list. Here is a simplified disaster planning checklist. Take a deep breath and start planning today.

DISASTER PLANNING CHECKLIST

Who are you planning for?

___ Self
___ Spouse/significant other
___ Children
___ Parents
___ Other

What do you need to plan for?

LEGAL PREPARATION:

___ Estate Planner/Lawyer (name, address, and phone)
___ Location of Legal Documents
___ Will
___ Trust or Living Will
___ Healthcare Proxy
___ Power of Attorney
___ Birth Certificates
___ Marriage License
___ Divorce Decree
___ Death Certificates

___ Special Arrangements for Dependent Children, Disabled Family Members, and Pets

INSURANCE PREPARATION:
___ Agent, Contact Number, Provider, Insured, Policy Number, and Value
___ Work-Provided Life Insurance
___ Whole Life Insurance
___ Term Life Insurance
___ Mortgage Insurance
___ Homeowner's Insurance
___ Umbrella Insurance
___ Flood Insurance
___ Car Insurance
___ RV Insurance
___ Boat Insurance
___ Other Vehicle Insurance

BANKING PREPARATION:
___ Bank Name, Branch, Contact, and Phone
___ Make sure all banking, safe deposit box, and financial accounts are in the name of the Family Trust.
___ Checking Account
___ Savings Account
___ ATM and Pin
___ Money Market
___ Safe Deposit Number, Joint Owner, Key Location
___ Investment Account

EMPLOYMENT / INVESTMENT / RETIREMENT / INCOME:

__ Employment Income
__ IRA
__ Roth IRA
__ 401K
__ Social Security
__ Brokerage Accounts
__ Stocks
__ Bonds
__ Commodities
__ Pension

PRE-PLANNING FOR DEATH:

__ Burial Plot
__ Mausoleum
__ Headstone
__ Funeral
__ Last Wishes in ICE File

PRE-PLANNING FOR MEDICAL DISASTER:

__ Insurance Carrier, Agent, and Contact Number
__ Medical Insurance
__ Medicare
__ Medicaid
__ RX Insurance
__ Secondary Insurance
__ Catastrophic Insurance
__ Disability Insurance (Short-Term/Long–Term)
__ Dental Insurance

__ Long-Term Care Insurance
__ Medical Savings Account
__ Home Health Care
__ DNR Order

PRE-PLANNING FOR NATURAL DISASTER:
__ **Create Your Family Disaster Plan.** Your safety
and the safety of your family is your number one
priority.
__ **Where to meet** in case you become separated
during the disaster.
__ **Identification** on each family member with
contact information for immediate family, ICE
contacts.
__ **Evacuation Plan.** If you are told to evacuate prior
to a disaster, do so. Where will you go? Shelter,
hotel, home of friend or other family member
__ **Non-Evacuation.** If you are staying in your home,
what is your plan if power is lost for days or
weeks?
__ Generator
__ Fuel
__ Lanterns
__ Radio
__ Medical supplies
__ Food
__ Water
__ **Communication.** Plan for communication with
each other and other family members outside of

the disaster area. Cell phones may or may not work and land lines may be down.

__ **Car.** Full tank of gas

__ **Disaster Kit.** Clothing and food for three to four days for each member of the family.

Basic Supplies:

__ Flashlight

__ Radio

__ Pillows

__ Blankets

__ Batteries

__ Rope

__ Duct tape

__ Toys

__ Other, etc.

Medical Supplies:

__ Equipment and supplies

__ Prescriptions

__ Supplements

__ Copies of Rx

__ Doctor contact information

__ Medical history

Documents:

__ Drivers' licenses

__ Passports

__ Birth certificates

__ Marriage license

___ Health insurance cards
___ ICE file (physical and electronic)

Pets:
___ Carrier for each pet
___ Food
___ Water
___ Medicine
___ Leash
___ Rabies vaccination records

Get your free Disaster Planning Checklist today at **www.TheCrisisPlanner.com.**

Take it one step at a time.

You will have your comprehensive plan in place before you know it.

It won't be hanging over your head like the elephant in the room.

You will have the peace of mind you so deserve and your family will have the protection they need.

19 GETTING IT TOGETHER

So now what's next?
You have followed the checklist and have completed all the steps.
Now you have to put it all together in one place where you or your family have quick, easy access.

That is what the **ICE (In Case of Emergency)** file is for. You should have a physical file in your file cabinet labeled ICE. You should have an electronic file on your computer labeled ICE. Finally you should have secure vault storage in the cloud and/or on a memory stick.

All of your key documents and information should be kept in your ICE file with additional copies in your safe deposit box and in cloud and/or memory stick storage. Keep in mind that, in case of death, your will is not likely to be read until weeks after your passing, so any instructions on your final wishes and information your family needs to know must be part of your ICE file.

It is not nearly as scary to put together as you think.

Why is that?

If you have followed the checklist from the previous chapter you have a lot of the work done already. It is just a matter of putting it together in one place.

What goes into your ICE file?

ICE Documents

- Bank Location and Account Numbers

- Online Banking Log-in Information

- Credit Card Numbers and Contact Phone Numbers

- Utility Account Numbers and Contact Phone Numbers

- Safe Deposit Box Number, Location, and Key

- Investment Accounts

- Legal Documents

- Insurance Documents

- Contact Names and Numbers for Lawyer, Accountant, Financial Advisor, and Insurance Agents

- Auto/Boat/Other Vehicle Titles

- Stock Certificates

- Bonds

- Gold/Silver/Platinum Bullion Location

- Appraisals for High-value Collectables

- Cash Stash Location

- Passport Numbers

- Copies of Driver's Licenses

- Instructions for Pets

- Funeral Requests and Information on Any Pre-paid Plans

- Last Wishes

- Computer Passwords for Accounts and Services

- Computer Backup on Memory Stick

Other Tips for ICE Files

Set up a list of ICE contacts on your cell phone. Emergency personnel are trained to look on your phone for ICE contacts.

Create a new contact:
- ICE Contact First and Last Name
- Relationship
- Cell Phone Number
- Home Phone Number

**Download your free
"ICE" (in case of emergency) Checklist today at**

www.TheCrisisPlanner.net

Now you are prepared for anything, and you have everything organized. You are ready for whatever disaster comes your way. Your family is protected and they know what to do.

Give yourself a big pat on the back.

20 ACTION, NOT REACTION

What it comes down to is taking action now.
Why now?
Now, because you have no time to waste.
Disaster can happen without warning. It can happen to you. It can happen anywhere, at any time.

Think about all the people without flood insurance who lost their homes or businesses during Superstorm Sandy. They lost everything they had worked for—their memories, their treasured belongings—and some lost their loved ones.

If they were not prepared, they paid a high price for that lack of preparation. Some would say, "How can you prepare for that kind of catastrophe? There was nothing that could have prevented it." They would be right at some level. The flood that occurred with the storm could not be changed. You could not prevent the loss of your home and everything in it.

WHAT PREPARATION CAN DO IS HELP YOU RECOVER FROM THE DISASTER.

All your important insurance coverage would be in place. All your important documents would be available so you could recover as quickly as possible.

Your family would be safe from such a storm. You would have your treasured photographs and memories.

The world will not be such a scary place if you take the time to plan.

When disaster strikes there is a physical component and an emotional component. The physical part of the disaster is the part over which you have some control. The way to have that control is to plan for disaster to minimize the impact on you and your family. Upheaval and chaos may still occur, but you can limit their impacts through effective planning. Rebuilding can begin sooner rather than later, and the chaos will not have control over you.

Once the physical side of disaster is addressed, you can move forward with the emotional healing that you cannot control. How you feel in the face of disaster is very personal. You may be angry, sad, lost, depressed, or confused.

All these emotions are normal. Being able to express them is part of the healing process. The emotional impact can be reduced by effective planning because you will be able to return to normal quicker with a plan than without one.

Rather than reacting, take action now.

21 SURVIVING THE AFTERMATH; LIFE REALLY DOES GO ON

There is life after disaster.

Even if you have not planned well. You will get through the disaster. You will survive. The disasters of life can be devastating. Your home could be destroyed or a loved one may die. Planning beforehand will help you get through a disaster with the least amount of pain. Your important papers and documents will be protected. Your wishes will be written down. The lines of communication will be open. This can be very empowering.

You will know what to do when you have a plan. The paperwork will go smoothly. You will not feel the profound panic of not knowing. Addressing the administrative side of the disaster with a clear plan behind it can bring things back under control as soon as possible.

Only when the physical side of dealing with the disaster is taken care of will you be able to start the healing process.

It is impossible to heal when your life is in chaos.

Control the chaos through effective planning and you have taken the first step to recovery.

What if you didn't have a plan before?
It is not too late. . . .
Create your new normal.

Take a deep breath and create a plan for recovery. Creating you recovery plan will put you back in control. Identify the steps necessary to create your new normal. You can never go back to where you were before the disaster. Things will be different. There will be things that cannot be replaced or people whose lives will never be the same. There may be losses of loved ones.

It will hurt.
You will cry.
You will be angry.
You will go on.
You will survive.
As you rebuild your life, the pain will slowly subside.
You will see the light at the end of the tunnel.
Your life will return to your new normal.
One day, you will wake up and know that not only were you able to survive the worst disaster you could imagine, but you were able to come out on the other side and thrive.

22 FINDING THE SILVER LINING

When disaster strikes, it is difficult to see beyond that moment when time seemed to stop.

You cannot see anything but the horror, the loss, or the chaos around you.

You can choose to wallow in your despair or you can choose to find something positive to focus on.

It is your choice.

I choose to look for the silver lining. It's not that I don't grieve my loss. I feel bad. I cry. I have the same feelings of loss. I just choose to know there was nothing I could have done to change what happened. I choose to know that I did my best to plan for the disaster before it happened.

I choose to look for something positive even in the worst possible situation.

I choose to find something to laugh about, even if it is myself.

I choose to find the silver lining. You can make that choice too.

Keep looking for the silver lining following a disaster. It's not always easy to find.

You may have to really search for it. It may not appear right away.

But, one day, you will see it.

A sliver of light will break through the clouds. The light will bring the smile back to your face, and the song back to your heart.

You will have faced your disaster and found your silver lining.

23 LAUGHTER IS THE BEST MEDICINE

Did you ever notice that the best comedy deals with some of the worst disasters?

When we face our most difficult times, the oppressive nature of the moment can drag us into despair. How do we stop our descent into depression? Often it is some silly, little thing that makes us smile. We suddenly see something so out of place that we start to laugh. We remember a moment shared with a loved one and share a secret giggle.

Laughter is the best medicine for our recovery.

Laughter allows helps us see the silver lining.

Laughter helps us to find our way back from disaster.

They say it takes sixty-four muscles to frown but only eight to smile. We are meant to be happy. We are supposed to smile. We need to laugh.

When you are finding your way back from a disaster, be it a natural disaster or a personal one, you may think you will never laugh again.

This is not possible.

You will laugh. When you least expect it, you will find yourself laughing. That laughter will release endorphins. Those endorphins will help expedite the healing process. Healing is both physical and emotional. Laughter works on both planes. Laugh at yourself, laugh at the situation, or laugh for the sake of it. Just laugh and you will feel better.

Watch a funny movie. Spend time with a child. You will laugh when they laugh. Bring the tissues. Once you release the laughter, you may laugh until you cry. Thank goodness for laughter.

Laughter truly is the best medicine for your recovery from disaster.

24 SHIT CANNED – WHAT'S BEHIND ME IS BEHIND ME

An Italian race-car driver, impeccably dressed, approaches his fine Italian race-car. He wears a long, flowing, white silk scarf. He slides into the car, pushes back his long, dark hair, and gives the scarf a flip. He reaches up and rips the rear-view mirror off the windshield. Looking at his companion, he says, "What's behind me is behind me."

This scene is from one of my favorite movies, "Gumball Rally."

I find this story relevant to the topic of disasters. Once a disaster has occurred, it IS behind you. You cannot rewind the tape for a do-over. You can only address the here and now.

What can you do today to recover?

What can you do to move forward?

What steps can you take to get your life back on track?

How will you heal today?

We all know from personal experience that "Shit Happens."

But, once it does happen, it is up to us to put it behind us,

And move forward.

25 POSITIVE OUTCOMES – MOVE FORWARD JOYFULLY

In this book, we have addressed all manner of disasters that we may face in life. I have laid out a planning blueprint for each disaster. While this is a book about disasters, it is also a book about preparing for the things that can happen and moving forward with our lives afterwards.

Life is so unpredictable. We face many things that are good and some that challenge our beliefs in God. There are little things that interrupt a day and big things that disrupt our lives.

SHIT HAPPENS. . . .

The impact of these disasters is largely in our control.

We can control how we prepare for them.

We can control how we react to them.

And we can control how we recover from them.

It is up to you to do your best preparation and planning, keep your sense of humor, and never give up on yourself.

You can create your positive outcome.

You just have to visualize it.

If you can see it clearly, it will happen.

Your recovery from disaster may be slow or fast.
You will recover at your own pace.

You MUST believe that recovery is possible.
Take it one day at a time.
Steadily, move forward
Find JOY in your life once again.

TAKE THE TIME TO PLAN WELL.

YOU WILL NOT ONLY SURVIVE,

YOU WILL THRIVE

AS YOU TURN THE PAGE

TO THE NEXT CHAPTER OF YOUR LIFE. . . .

RESOURCES

WWW.THECRISISPLANNER.COM
WWW.THECRISISPLANNER.NET
NATURAL DISASTER RESOURCES

- FEMA.GOV

- STATE/COUNTY/OR TOWN DISASTER PLAN

- THEWEATHERCHANNEL.COM

- NOAA.GOV

- WWW.READY.GOV

- LOCAL POLICE OR FIRE DEPARTMENT

- REDCROSS.ORG

- EMERGENCY ALERT NETWORK

- NATIONAL FLOOD INSURANCE PROGRAM (NFIP) at USA.GOV

MEDICAL RESOURCES

- MEDICARE.GOV

- HEALTHCARE.GOV

- STATE HEALTHCARE EXCHANGE

- MEDICAID-HELP.ORG

- YOUR LOCAL VISITING NURSE SERVICE

- SUPPORT AND COUNSELING SERVICES

- MEDICALGUARDIAN.COM

- MEDICALALERTCOMPARISON.COM

- LIFEALERT.COM

- SOCIAL SERVICES

SOCIAL SECURITY AND DISABILITY RESOURCES

- SOCIALSECURITY.GOV

- WWW.SSA.GOV/DISABILITYSSI/SSI.HTML

- AFLAC.COM

MILITARY RESOURCES

- U.S. DEPARTMENT OF VETERANS AFFAIRS

- PLAN MY DEPLOYMENT, MILITARY
  COMMUNITY AND FAMILY POLICY FACT
  SHEET

- MILITARY ONESOURCE DEPLOYMENT
  RESOURCES

- REAL WARRIORS CAMPAIGN RESOURCES
- USAA.COM
- ACTIVE DUTY SINGLE PARENTS DEPLOYMENT READINESS CHECKLIST
- MILITARY ONE SOURCE TIPS
- OPERATION MILITARY KIDS
- DEPLOYMENT HEALTH & FAMILY READINESS LIBRARY
- COMING HOME: A GUIDE FOR SERVICE MEMBER RETURNING FROM MOBILIZATION/DEPLOYMENT

FINANCIAL RESOURCES

- MONEYOVER55.ABOUT.COM
- 5 MISTAKES THAT LEAD TO IDENTIFY THEFT

LEGAL RESOURCES

- 10 QUESTIONS FOR AN ELDER LAW ATTORNEY
- ELDER LAW ANSWERS
- ESTATE.FINDLAW.COM

SECURITY RESOURCES

- LIFELOCK.COM

- LEGALSHIELD.COM

- AARP ID PROTECTION

- IDTHEFT.ABOUT.COM

- CARBONITE

- KEEPER (PASSWORD MANAGER AND DIGITAL VAULT)

- HOME SECURITY SYSTEM/MONITORED

CREDIT REPORTING RESOURCES

- EQUIFAX.COM

- EXPERIAN.COM

- TRANSUNION.COM

HOME REPAIR RESOURCES

- ABOUT.COM/PLANNINGSENIORS

- ANGIESLIST.COM

- HOMEADVISOR.COM

- HOME WARRANTY PLANS

OTHER RESOURCES

- IRS.GOV

- AARP.COM

- CONSUMERREPORTS.ORG